THE 7 Secrets of Awakening the Highly Effective Four-Hour Giant, Today

"*The Gang Writes a Self-Help Book*"

IT'S ALWAYS SUNNY IN PHILADELPHIA

THE 7 Secrets of Awakening the Highly Effective Four-Hour Giant, Today

CHARLIE, MAC, DENNIS, SWEET DEE, AND FRANK WROTE THIS BOOK

TITAN BOOKS

It's Always Sunny in Philadelphia:
The 7 Secrets of Awakening the Highly Effective Four-Hour Giant, Today
Print edition ISBN: 9781783298396
E-book edition ISBN: 9781783298402

Published by Titan Books
A division of Titan Publishing Group Ltd.
144 Southwark Street, London SE1 0UP

First edition January 2015
6 8 10 9 7 5

www.titanbooks.com

A CIP catalogue record for this title is available from the British Library.

Printed and bound by CPI Group (UK) Ltd, Croydon, CR0 4YY

To Jamie Nelson, who's swimming in heaven, and
Dooley, who would've loved our party mansion

Contents

Legal Notice xiii

Introduction xvii

PART I

Relationships

1 S.I.N.N.E.D.: The Reverse D.E.N.N.I.S. System 3

2 Discrimination Prejudice 7

3 Other People's Children Are Disgusting
Shit-Monsters 10

4 Charlie Kelly: Pursun Ecspurt 13

*Dennis Reynolds: Best Friend,
Best Person* 13

*Dennis Reynolds: Worst Friend,
Worst Person* 14

*Dennis and Deandra Are a Couple
of Ungrateful Twats* 16

 17

5 The Gang Answers Your Questions About Love 19

6 Banging Through the Years 25

7 Devotion 30

8 I Beat Marriage and So Can You 34

9 Here's How Straight I Am 39

10 You Gotta Have a Sidekick 41

11 A Man and His Horse: The Story of Peter
Nincompoop 44

QUIZ QUORNER 46

PART II

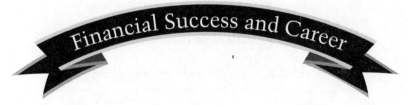

Financial Success and Career

12 The Bone-Crushing Power of Words 57

13 Conflict Resolution 60

14 Getting Rich off Your Kids 63

15 How to Make Millions as an Actress and Quit Your
Crappy Bar Job 67

16 Hans Wermhatt: Drem Bastid 71

17 Steal Your Way to a Better Life 76

18 Refuse to Relent 79

19 Charlie Work and How to Avoid It 82

20 The Way of the Wild Card 84

QUIZ QUORNER 87

PART III

Fashion and Personal Grooming

21 Makeup: A Man's Game 97

22 America: Love It or Sleeve It 100

23 The Nightman 103

24 Blackface Versus Whiteface 107

25 How to Look Like a Giant Bird 112

26 When Charlie Met Holland Oates 115

QUIZ QUORNER 122

PART IV

Health and Diet

27 All-Time Top Physiques 131

28 Recipe Corner: Rum Ham 139

29 Imagining a New You 142

30 Recipe Corner: Blue Tea à la Charlie 147

31 Aluminum Humor 149

32 Recipe Corner: Charlie's Cheese Recipes 152

33 Recipe Corner: Chicken Soup for the 'Hole 155

34 Recipe Corner: Raccoon Steak 158

35 Spiritual Nutrition 163

36 How to Stage an Intervention 166

QUIZ QUORNER 175

PART V

Survival Skills

37 Shushing People: A Dangerous Game 187

38 A Guide to Keeping Birds as Pets 190

39 How to Strike Out with a Porn Star
Like Dennis Did 193

40 When the Bums Come for Us 199

41 Overcoming Overcoming Trauma 203

42 Soon I Will Rule You All 209

43 Rat Py To Owld 211

44 Is This Heaven? 214

45 What's Everyone's Problem Today? 216

46 It's Wrong to Poison People 218

QUIZ QUORNER 221

Afterword 231

Acknowledgments 235

LEGAL NOTICE

Dear Reader,

On behalf of Titan Books, I would like to extend my sincerest apologies to anyone who has squandered their hard-earned money on the purchase of *The 7 Secrets of Awakening the Highly Effective Four-Hour Giant, Today.*

At the time of this printing, the "words" that fill this "book" have cost our company roughly $133,744.55. Our finance department has determined that we must actually publish this title in order to prevent it from costing us much more in extensive legal fees. While I was prepared to face the "authors" in court, it was deemed fiscally irresponsible, even if morally sound.

One advance reviewer of *The 7 Secrets of Awakening the Highly Effective Four-Hour Giant, Today* correctly described it as "less a work of 'self-help' than of 'helping yourself.'" Another called it "the most offensive and unhelpful book since Miley Cyrus's memoir *Miles to Go*." The book is, and will remain, a professional humiliation for our company. Even in this so-called digital age, we still pride ourselves on professionalism, attention to detail, and unwavering commitment to publishing quality books that meet the highest industry standards. Sadly, we have fallen short of that goal in this case.

You may be wondering how Titan Books was compelled to publish something so totally devoid of any creative or artistic merit. I feel it is only fair to proceed with complete honesty, and our lawyers agree. In the spring of 2014 an executive editor (who has since entered a long-term treatment facility for substance abuse) visited an establishment in Philadelphia called Paddy's Pub. We presume her intent was some sort of social anthropology research.

There she met a custodian named Charles Kelly, who immediately committed the tort of civil fraud by identifying himself as the bar's proprietor. Over the course of several hours, Mr. Kelly plied said editor with large amounts of alcohol, later estimated to be at least five times the legal limit for the operation of an automobile. In addition, we have reason to believe that significant amounts of nonmedical marijuana were consumed. Also, apparently at the urging of Mr. Kelly, our editor was enticed to "huff" Scotchgard and model airplane glue. While she was thus intoxicated, our editor—who, I should note, was going through a painful divorce at the time—became convinced that Mr. Kelly's "unique life advice" might translate to a wide commercial audience. She left an impassioned, and slurred, voice mail message for me on my office line claiming that Mr. Kelly was a "self-help guru" on the scale of Dr. Oz and she was ready to sign him before another publishing house could swoop in "like a giant blond bird." In fact, Mr. Kelly is a semiliterate alcoholic janitor with severe emotional problems.

Though clearly and severely impaired, the editor, still acting as common-carrier legal agent of Titan Books under Pennsylvania law, made the unfortunate and costly decision to offer Mr. Kelly a substantial book deal "on the spot." Using even more chicanery, Mr. Kelly managed to convince the editor to include several of his cohorts in the misbegotten deal as well. Hence the participation of Messrs. Dennis Reynolds, Ronald McDonald, and Frank Reynolds, along with the individual identified as Ms. Deandra Reynolds. We have since taken measures to secure all publishing contracts at our central offices in Manhattan and have included a line invalidating any contract signed under the influence of airplane glue.

The 7 Secrets of Awakening the Highly Effective Four-Hour Giant, Today is not in any way representative of the caliber of books our readers have come to expect from us, and for that we are immeasurably sorry. Following the "advice" contained herein could get you arrested, maimed, or killed. I repeat, <u>do not</u> under any circumstances take any of the advice offered in this book. In fact, things will probably go better for you if you just toss it in the trash right now. Don't even worry about finishing reading this apology. I am not a proud man, and I simply want you to have a full, enjoyable life.

While we cannot legally offer refunds at this time, it may be of some comfort to know that all parties involved in the acquisition of *The 7 Secrets of Awakening the Highly Effective Four-Hour Giant, Today* are no longer in the employ of Titan Books. As for the "authors," we offer no comment on their current whereabouts, but based upon the return address of harassing postcards we continue to receive about "$$'s O'd 2 us," we believe it to be Philadelphia.

With kindest regards and deepest sympathies,

Ray Curtis
Publisher (Retired)
Titan Books

INTRODUCTION

By Mac

Hello there. My name is Mac and I am the undisputed leader of my "gang" of friends.* In your hands you hold the incredible book we just wrote, and we'd like to thank you for having the good sense to purchase it. Or most of you anyway. If you haven't purchased it and are just dicking around in the bookstore like a tease, picking up books and bending the covers and getting the pages all creasy, then we'd like it if you stopped reading right now and put this book back on the shelf, you cheap sonofabitch. Way to not change your life, buddy! You should be ashamed.

Are all the cheap sonofabitches gone? Good. Let's get to the introducting! Reader, meet *The 7 Secrets of Awakening the Highly Effective Four-Hour Giant, Today*. You guys are going to be pals. This book will teach you things that will make your life better in literally fives of ways. In fact, you have already learned the first thing this book is going teach you: that nothing worthwhile in life is free. This book, for example, cost you like $17 plus tax. (Unless you're still freeloading in the store.† Or you got it as a gift, in which case, why don't you just move to Canada if you like handouts so much?)

---

* Suck it, Dennis.
† In which case, seriously, sack up and go buy it already. If you can't change your own life, the least you can do is change ours.

But as I was saying, me and my friends wrote this book to help people.* It's who we are. We're givers. Some of you may be wondering what makes people like us qualified to write a self-help book. I'd like nothing more than to get into all that, but as it turns out there's some litigation pending at the moment and on the advice of Charlie's uncle Jack I'm not at liberty to talk about certain matters related to how this book came to be. Needless to say, though, we are *totally* somebodies and we're totally qualified to be book writers and world-renowned fixers of other people's broken pathetic lives. Otherwise, *ergo quo ipso,* you wouldn't be holding this thing in your hands, would you? Book executives don't spend butt-tons of cash churning out a bunch of crap by complete assholes nobody gives a shit about. That's a TV executive's job.

Since I can't talk about how the book came to be, let me break the title down for you. First off, the more observant among you may have noticed that we promise seven secrets in the title, yet the book contains only five sections. The reason for this is simple, but it's a secret. In fact it's the first secret of the book. Oh man, you would think it was hilarious if I told you. So ironic, yet so perfect. It's just so *us,* y'know? Anyway, the less questions you ask about the number seven in the title the better, because we're not going to tell you, and it's definitely not because people just love the number seven for no rational reason.† Besides, five sections is a *lot* less work than seven, and one of the secrets to finishing what you start is to not start so many things. That's a bonus secret for you, right up front. I think it's fair to say that we don't skimp on the secrets around here.

The "awakening" part is pretty straightforward. Most numbnuts are content to sleepwalk their way through life, and the only way they're ever going to amount to anything more than human leeches on American resources is if someone blasts 'em in the face with a white-hot load

---

* And to make a bunch of money and be famous.

† Yeah, and it's just a coincidence that seven is how many minutes you should spend blasting your abs, and the number of dwarves Snow White hangs out with, and the first movie ever to star Gwyneth Paltrow's severed head.

of Truth.* We are those someones, this book is our white-hot load, the words inside are the Truth, and the eyes you read them with are your face. You might want to have a paper towel handy, because you're about to have Truth all over it.

Dennis said we should put "highly effective" in there because it's 2015 and regular old "effective" doesn't cut it anymore. The "four-hour" thing was Frank's idea. He said something about how people want something substantial, and that means it has to take a while, but not so long that they have to spend their whole lives doing it. It boils down to this: Everyone has four hours, but if changing their entire life from top to bottom takes any longer than that, they'll lose interest.

The part about the giant was all me. It's a subtle reference to my physique. It's no secret that I've been bulking up lately, and not just on the glamour muscles. I've been blasting my core like a madman† as an inspiration for all the flabby slobs out there who wouldn't know a deltoid from an Altoid. If that's you, don't worry, we go over the exact difference in the book.‡ By the time you finish reading this thing you'll be super ripped, just like me. It's all part of the service.

All right, you feeling introduced? Let the healing begin! Besides me, you'll be hearing from my associates Dennis, Charlie, and Frank. You might also hear some high-pitched squawking that sounds like a giant bird trapped in a paper shredder. That's Dee. You'll know her pieces by the typos. It's hard for her to find keyboards big enough to accommodate her massive bison fingers.

Just remember, if you finish the book and your whole life hasn't changed, that's normal. It's not you. Just head back to the bookstore and buy another copy and start over at the beginning. Remember, change starts with you . . .§

---

* Oh yeah, capital T, baby. We are not messing around.
† In seven-minute increments, naturally.
‡ We don't, but don't tell chubby.
§ . . . buying a whole lot of copies of this book.

PART I

Relationships

S.I.N.N.E.D.:

The Reverse

D.E.N.N.I.S. System

By Dee

There are so so so so many things about my shitface brother that bug the shit out of me, from his delusions of grandeur about his looks to his vain pretensions about his artistic ability to his megadickalomania (that's when you think you have a huge penis but you don't). Dennis is, quite simply, the most grandeuristically delusional dickbag on the planet, and nothing illustrates this better than his psychotic belief in his powers of seduction . . . or what he refers to as the D.E.N.N.I.S. System. It works—or, rather, doesn't work*—like this:

---

* Oh, ZING.

> # D----> "Demonstrate Value"
> # E ----> "Engage Physically"
> # N----> "Nurture Dependence"
> # N----> "Neglect Emotionally"
> # I ----> "Inspire Hope"
> # S ----> "Separate Entirely"

See? Just terrible. It's pretty much the most sociopathic and selfish thing you can imagine. I mean, haven't we evolved just a little as a species from this kind of empty, primitive, rut-oriented behavior? I mean, his system doesn't involve money at any step. Which is probably why he still has a roommate, while I'm living fat in my own apartment.* To prove just how stuck in the Stone Age the D.E.N.N.I.S. System is, I came up with a system of my own that works way better than his. Allow me to take the D.E.N.N.I.S. System and turn that frown around. Ladies and germs, I present the S.I.N.N.E.D. System. It goes a little something like this.

Once you've got a target in your sights, take the following steps:

S—"Size Him Up" (His Wallet, Not His Dick). You can
do this a number of ways. One of my favorites is pretending to
nuzzle his cheek while he's using the ATM, then "accidentally"

---

* It's just an expression. I am not, nor will I ever be, fat. And my feet are quite normal for a woman my height. Which is a normal, many would say quite attractive, height.

hitting the "Check Balance" button. If you have a few days, do a little Internet search on him to get some personal info and order a free credit check. Or hire hackers to break into his bank account. If you get that far, you can just have them transfer out some cash, and you don't even need to go on the date. Alternately, if you find he's a broke loser you don't have to go on the date either. Does your system have early outs, Dennis? Thought not.

I—"Isolate." You do not want other gold-digging bitches
dipping their pans in your river. Once you've established he's solvent and you go on that first date, tie up all of his free time. If you catch him looking at anyone else, fake a sprained ankle. Sometimes you'll need to go so far as to actually sprain your ankle. Basically the idea here is to tie him up completely for a couple weeks without having sex with him. You're going to need to be a little creative here, but a combination of injuries and "lady problems" usually does the trick for me.

N—"Now Bang Him." This is pretty
straightforward. At the two-week mark you can finally give in and bang him. This needs to be a spectacular one. Best bang of this guy's life. Really go hog wild and give him a show. Blast Bad Company and get gritty, because this bozo's going to be paying for it for a while.

N—"Neutralize Sexual Advances." You've
given him a taste of the candy; now it's time to leave him begging for more. That means it's back to the mystery ailments and yeast infections, but this time, you need to recuperate at his place. They're painting/fumigating/delousing yours, remember? Play up the pitiful angle and wait for him to trust you enough to leave you alone in his apartment while he's at work. Sucker.

E—"Empty All Accounts." While you're "sleeping off the flu" at his place, you'll actually be scouring his apartment for online passwords and ATM codes. If you run into any snags, go ahead and use roofie hypnosis on him.

D—"Dee Wins!" Because I get all the sucker's money, and I get out. And I'm happy and well-adjusted and all you turkeys like Dennis can suck it because I know the key to true and lasting happiness with a man. The key is his checking account. Have fun with your vapid and unfulfilling banging strategy, Dennis. Give me a call when you can afford your own apartment.

Discrimination

Prejudice

By Mac

F irst of all, let's get one thing out of the way. This section is not about black people. It's about relationships. If I say it's about black people then I'll get all kinds of static from the PC police about how I'm a racist. Let me just say it once and for all. I'm "not racist," okay? And this piece is "not about black people."

Happy now, black people? Okay, everyone else, keep reading.

There's been an awful lot of talk in recent years about how everyone's equal and no one should discriminate. Well I'm here to tell you that's a crock of shit. And ah-ah-ah-ah, don't get up on your moral high horse, okay? This has nothing to do with race. I tell people I voted for Obama all the time. And by "people" I mean black chicks. And by "voted for" I mean half-contemplated giving enough of a shit to figure out how to vote before moving on to something more important. Like fighting crime. (Oh, what, you love crime now?)

So let's get something straight right off the bat: Not everyone is equal. It's a basic, but still apparently uncomfortable, fact that some of us are just set apart from others at birth. Is it Carl Weathers's fault that he is genetically superior to those around him, much like myself? No! Is it Sylvester Stallone's fault that his extra-advanced superbrain was able to produce the script for *Rocky* in just twenty hours (eerily echoing the epic session that resulted in *Lethal Weapon 5*)? Absolutely not! And it's ridiculous that these two great men have spent so much time dealing with the whiners and losers and cripples who say, "Oooh, I'm uncomfortable with these men and their taut rippling muscles. Their perfect physiques make me feel inadequate." When you're truly free of PREJUDICE (yeah, I said it), you realize that it's okay to become aroused at the sight of another man's sick lats, especially when that man is Dolph Lundgren. That kind of excellence should give you inspiration and maybe a half chub. (A fitness boner is nothing to be ashamed of.) What it shouldn't do is make you call the NAACP or the ACLU or NAMBLA or whoever. I can't keep track of all those liberal organizations and their fancy letter-names.

But before we go any further, I have a confession to make: I might have lied to you a little earlier when I said this chapter wasn't about black people. Because I said it wasn't and then I brought up Carl Weathers (who is openly black) in a positive context. Oh! Who's prejudiced now? You. Against me. Because I discriminate.

That's right. You, my friend, are prejudiced against discrimination. Yeah, I said it.

I went ahead and looked up "discrimination" in the dictionary, and do you know what it means? "The ability to understand that one thing is different from another thing." Yeah! So apparently if I happen to notice that, say, Sylvester Stallone's immense, cut bulk is different from Arnold's insanely massed-up physique, suddenly I'm the bad guy? They're not the same, you guys. Two different giant dudes blasting you in the face is just that—two different giant dudes blasting you in the face. Pretend otherwise and you're just fooling yourself. No, it is NOT all the same in the dark.

But I can hear the whiners already. "Mac, Mac, you're ignoring the true meaning of discrimination. The one that has to do with ugly truths about America and its history." Okay, fine. Let's go there. I think we all know there's a deeper meaning to the word "discrimination." And to see what it is, all you have to do is break it down. There's three clear parts to "dis-crimi-nation."

"Dis" is easy. It means you want to dis whatever comes next.

"Crimi" is the Greek root for the word "Cry me," as in "Cry me a river." It's basically sarcastic taunting. A loose translation would be "I'm a little bitch. Watch me cry to my mommy."

"Nation," obviously, is this great nation of ours.

Now let's unbreak it down. Dis Cry-Me Nation. When you use discrimination you're dissing the idea that someone would tell AMERICA that it's a little baby that should go crying to its mama. So I'm proud to be a discriminator. Because I would never tell the United States (the UNITED STATES!) that it was some little bitch boy. Because it isn't. How could it be? This country practically invented getting blasted in the face by big beautiful black men like Carl Weathers. And if hating that is wrong, I don't want to be right.

If you hate discrimination, you hate America. And if you hate America, you'd better hope you and I don't ever meet in a dark alley. Because I will pound your ass so hard you won't know what hit you.

Other People's
Children Are
Disgusting
Shit-Monsters

By Dee

I ran into a friend from high school named Suzette at the mall the other day. Okay, it might be a stretch to call her a friend, since we always had a fairly one-sided relationship. There was me—the most popular girl in school—and then there was homely little Suzette, totally wishing she was me.

The dictionary defines "adoration" as "strong admiration or devotion," but they really ought to add something about what a total pain in the ass it can be for the ones who are being adored, and also something about how pathetic people like Suzette are. Believe me, when I saw her coming over to me in the food court the other day I just wanted to disappear because I knew I was going to have to sit there and listen to her go on and on about how great I look and how smart I am and how totally sorry she still is for having gotten pissed at me senior year for banging my English teacher. She's just touchy about it because it was her dad. Whatever, it was cool and I kind of have a thing for authority figures.

But I almost shit myself when I saw the two little brats she was dragging along behind her. Turns out that by some miracle, ugly-ass Suzette got some sorry-ass douchebag to marry her *and* knock her up. So all you lonely trolls out there, take heart. There's hope for you yet, no matter how shrewlike and malformed you are.

So now instead of having to endure an ungodly hour of her chewing my friggin' ear off about how awesome I am, instead I had to pretend to be interested while Suzette gushed about little Shitstain and her brother Asswipe. I don't know how old they are. I think she said four and six. Hard to tell through all the rolls of chub. You know how they say the apple doesn't fall too far from the tree? Well apparently neither do the Twinkies and cheesesteaks and soft pretzels. I wouldn't say they're spitting images of their plus-sized mom. It's more like swallowing images. As in, everything in sight.

Oh, what's that? You think I'm being mean? On the contrary, I'm just being honest. The fact of the matter is, I'm not alone in thinking other people's kids suck. Everyone thinks that, even people who have kids of their own. *Especially* people who have kids of their own.

Because everyone wants *their* progeny to be the ones who get rich and famous and get on a reality show and end up best friends with Tom Cruise. Parents think that if they just push her hard enough their delicate snowflake Madyson* will grow up to be a winner. The kind of superlative being who uses fancy words like "progeny" and who would never be caught dead hanging out with some loser like Suzette unless

* Or insert future stripper name here.

in her magnanimous awesomeness she did it because she felt sorry for her. But trust me, these parents are living in a fantasy world. In actuality their kids suck as much as everyone else's. If your kids are even vaguely accomplished, they're a threat to everyone's carefully constructed fantasies, which means they suck. And if they're lazy, smelly, whiny little brats (more likely), then they just suck outright. It's really unavoidable.

So unless you can train your kid to carry my groceries, kick my jerkoff brother in the nuts, or score me crack so I don't have to go to neighborhoods that scare me, keep them out of my face and stop telling me dumb stories about them. Of course, if you do end up training your kid to do any of those things, definitely let me know. I've always had a soft spot for kids.

4

Charlie Kelly:

Pursun Ecspurt

Hey, guys. Dennis here. We were talking about the relationships portion of the book and Charlie was having a little trouble composing his thoughts on paper. He asked me if I could help him out. Being a natural giver I, of course, said yes. And then he sprung it on me that he wanted the section to be about me! Specifically about what a great all-around person I am and how unfailingly helpful I've been to him throughout our friendship. It weirded me out at first, but it isn't really that weird when you think about it. Anyway, here goes. Hope you enjoy. I know I did.

DENNIS REYNOLDS: BEST FRIEND, BEST PERSON

By Charlie (as told to Dennis)

Dennis is the sleekest, most catlike man ever to roam the earth. Back in caveman times they spoke of a prophecy—one day a man would come, not to rule, not to enslave, but to inspire. He would not be an arrogant man. He would not be a wealthy man. He would walk the earth with the grace of a swan and the plumage of an eagle, yet he would mix with the ordinaries for the sole purpose of inspiring them with his cheekbones, his shapely calves, and his innate sense of style.

The prophecy also foretold that one day he would meet me, Charlie Kelly, a lowly janitor at the blessed bar run by the aforementioned incredible chosen one, Dennis, and several other people whose names have been lost to the mists of time. I'm happy to have known you, Dennis. You took pity on a poor, wretched soul by letting me tell people you were my friend. I've never known a better person and I think I never will.

Oh, hey, what's up, y'all. Sweet Dee at your service with a little help for my buddy Charlie. Seems he got a little overwhelmed with composing all these fancy words and wanted "the smartest person [he] know[s]" to help him out with it. So here I am. Helping. Cuz that's just what I do. Anyway, he thinks he might not have been clear in the last piece he did with Dennis's help and wanted to make sure his message got across.

DENNIS REYNOLDS: WORST FRIEND, WORST PERSON

By Charlie (as told to Dee)

Dennis is the sleekest, most catlike man ever to roam the earth. Back in caveman times they spoke of a prophecy—one day a man would come, not to rule, not to enslave, and, most importantly, not to inspire. He would be an arrogant man. He would be a wealthy man. He would think he walked the earth with the grace of a swan and the plumage of an eagle, yet he'd really just be a lame asshole who secretly videotaped the skanks he banged.

See, here's the thing: Dennis is a dumb-face. His face is actually dumb. Not his brain. His face. Dumb like a bag of hammers that never finished elementary school. Stupid like a thing that's really really super stupid all the time. And mean. Not his face this time, just his whole Dennis. All of the Dennis is all of the mean all of the time to all of his sisters. He actually only has one sister, but she is really really nice and only wants the best for him and has always been there, from the beginning, to lend him money and do his homework and calm him down when he came to her to just cry and cry and cry because Maureen Ponderosa dumped him for the fourth time.

But does Dennis ever do anything nice for his beautiful sister? No, he doesn't. He just calls her ugly and says she has gigantic thumbs and tells her she should go hang out at the beach because that's where all the other gigantic weird-looking birds are. No, Dennis is a bad man and no one likes him. They only feel sorry for him, and everyone should remember that forever.

Oh man, did I ever have a weird day. I was under the bridge and Duncan got all territorial about the syringe pile again. Like I haven't put any syringes on that pile. Asshole. This is Frank, by the way. Frank Reynolds. Anyway, Charlie grabbed me outside the bar and told me he was worried that Deandra and Dennis have been jerking him around with this whole book thing. Typical. Those two wouldn't know how to do a friend an honest favor if they had a gun to their heads. Actually, you know, that's not a bad experiment. I'm going to have to try that. But let me take care of this first. Charlie asked me to set the record straight about how he feels about friendship.

DENNIS AND DEANDRA ARE A COUPLE

OF UNGRATEFUL TWATS

By Charlie (as told to Frank)

Let me tell you about my good friends Dennis and Deandra Reynolds. They are a couple of ungrateful twats. Did you know that Dennis's stepfather saved his butt by buying into the bar he owns and Dennis has never even once said so much as "Thank you," let alone "Hey, Frank, you're more like a father than a stepfather the way you bail me out all the time, come on, let's go down to the whorehouse and get you an 'around the world' on me." What a twat.

And Deandra, don't get me started on her. First of all, she's not the most ladylike, but that's probably because she's not Frank's actual daughter. If she were, she'd be more debonair, more worldly, and have a little meat on her bones. Sort of like a female Frank. You know, handsome. In a lady kind of way. And even though her stepfather owns part of the bar and is basically responsible for her having a job, does Frank ever get so much as a how-de-do on Father's Day? Or his birthday? Or when one of his favorite whores croaks? No, it's always "Put down the gun, Frank," "Wipe the mayonnaise off your forehead, Frank," and "No one wants to see your dong, Frank." Everyone wants to see Frank's dong. It's a great dong.

Anyway, they're both ungrateful assholes. And I should know because I'm Charlie Kelly and I wrote this and all Frank did was write everything down perfect, just the way I said it.

4 ƎVRY 1

BYE CAT

MAC 🎖️🤝 GOOD MAN

MAC TƎACH CAT TO ⚔ CAT NAMƎ

👤← CAT

MAC TEACH CAT SPƎLL CAT.

EDITOR'S NOTE: When we first received the manuscript we had difficulty parsing the sections Mr. Kelly wrote himself until we uncovered a key piece of information. Apparently coauthor Mr. McDonald thought it would be funny to "teach" Charlie to write his name and then told him it was spelled C-A-T. Titan Books does not condone this type of manipulative behavior and we only reproduce the material shown here due to contractual obligation.

The Gang Answers
Your Questions
About Love

By the Gang

EDITOR'S NOTE: This chapter was transcribed from one of many audio recordings that were submitted in lieu of actual written copy.

Mac: Okay, hi, we're rolling. This is *The 7 Secrets of Awakening the Highly Effective Four-Hour Giant, Today,* part I, chapter five, in which we will answer your burning questions about love. I'm Mac, and with me are Dennis, Dee, and Charlie.

Charlie: And I'm Charlie.

Dennis: Are you sure it's chapter five?

Mac: Um . . . yeah, I'm positive.

Dennis: I thought the essay I wrote about what I learned from my marriage was chapter five.

Mac: We decided to cut that, remember?

Dennis: What are you talking about?

Dee: We're talking about your terrible essay. Which we decided to cut.

Dennis: I don't seem to remember any discussion about it.

Dee: That might have had something to do with the seventeen beers you had that day.

Mac: Or the fact that we decided it while you were in the bathroom. We figured it was best to just take a quick vote. It was pretty much unanimous.

Dennis: Charlie, you voted against me?

Charlie: I had to. They kept calling me a nanny mouse.

Dennis: A what?

Charlie: A nanny mouse. They were both pointing at me and saying, "You nanny mouse, you nanny mouse," over and over until I agreed to vote against you.

Dennis: Oh Jesus. Seriously? Look, he's crying now, you monsters.

Charlie: I am not a nanny mouse!

Mac: We did this to him? You're the one who wrote the boringest essay in the history of writing boring things down.

Dennis: Oh come on! It's a brilliant essay. You're just intimidated by my penetrating insights into the myriad challenges and subtle complexities of the world's most cherished cultural—

Charlie: Booooooooooorrrrrring!

Mac: Dude, you were married for one friggin' day.

Dennis: What's that supposed to mean?

Dee: It means you don't know shit about marriage, dickwad!

Dennis: Oh, look what learned to talk—a lonely bird-monster whose longest meaningful relationship was with a violet dildo.

Dee: Oh, goddamn it! Don't you bring Steven into this!

Dennis: I'll have you assholes know that I gave everything I had to try and make that marriage work. Not a day goes by that I don't grieve over the dissolution of our union and the shattered promise of love everlasting with Pamela.

Mac: Maureen.

Dennis: You see that? That's how upset I am! The pain was so great I repressed the name of my long-lost . . . then found . . . then lost again love . . . ah . . . oh . . .

Dee: Seriously?

Dennis: It's on the tip of my tongue . . .

Mac: Maureen.

Dennis: Maureen! Good old Maureen. Used to call her "Een." When we'd bang I'd ask her, "Hey, how about some more, Een?" And then I'd give her some more, if you know what I'm saying.

Charlie: That's what marriage is like?

Dennis: Sure is, buddy.

Charlie: Sounds pretty awesome.

Dee: Ew.

Dennis: Built-in sexual wordplay is the best foundation for a long-term union.

Dee: Is that right? Well then, Dennis, tell me. If you have such high regard for the *sacred* institution of marriage, then why did you bang Maureen Ponderosa on the day she was supposed to marry Liam McPoyle?

Dennis: Is that what this is about? Because there's a very simple answer. See, she'd gotten a giant pair of fake—

Charlie: I think I can provide some insight into Dennis's behavior, Dee.

Dennis: Charlie, it's really not—

Charlie: Just let me finish! Okay. Geez. Who knows what tomorrow brings? In a world, few hearts survive. All I know is the way I feel. When it's real, I keep it alive. The road is long. There are mountains in our way. But we climb a step every day.

Mac: Dude, that's the theme song from *An Officer and a Gentleman*.

Charlie: Does that make it any less true? [*sings*] Love lift us up where we belong . . .

Mac: We can't use stuff like that in the book. It's plagiarism.

Charlie: It's a movie, not a play, dude! So, yeah, don't think it's going to be a problem.

Dennis: Mac's right, we need to use new material we create ourselves. Like my essay.

Dee: Gonna go ahead and stop you right there. We need to use new material we create ourselves, but it's also important that it doesn't immediately put the reader into an irreversible coma.

Dennis: Wow. That really stings.

Dee: Oh come on. You've never loved anything in this world apart from yourself.

Mac: That is not true! Dennis loves me with the fury of a thousand suns.

[long pause]

Charlie: Oh man, this is awkward.

Dee: Yeah, I feel like my skin's gonna turn inside out I'm cringing so much.

Mac: Dennis? Where are you going? Don't you walk out on me without saying a . . . god DAMN IT!

[sound of door slamming]

Dee: Phew. Good job, Mac.

Mac: I know. He totally went for it.

Charlie: He was really holding up the process, wasn't he?

Mac: As usual. Okay, so what were we talking about again? Love?

Dee: Dennis's terrible essay.

Mac: Oh yeah. You know what, I bet if we just turned in a tape recording of this conversation it'd be more entertaining than that piece of dog crap.

Dee: Oh, that's great. Imagine if we did that.

6

Banging Through

the Years

By Frank

O kay, so the kids asked me to contribute to their little book. Said they needed material on relationships. Oh, what do I know about relationships, I've only had about seventeen million of 'em.

See, I've been gettin' with broads since before I could crawl. Shit, my earliest memory is waking up with my mom Tina's tit in my mouth. How messed up is that? That was around the age of six or so. I don't know, my memory ain't too good anymore. I just know it was some real traumatic shit when she finally cut me off. They say a man's first love is his mother, and it's true, but boy did she break my heart when she finally cut off my milk supply.

Where was I? Oh yeah. Some people say that all the bangin' I did was just a way for me to compensate for my "severe Oedipus complex," but I know the truth. After I got sent off to the nitwit school I knew I was damaged goods in the eyes of a lot of broads, so I felt like if I banged enough, word would spread that ol' Frankie boy wasn't such a bad egg after all.

But don't worry. I learned an important lesson from all my adventures with women: They all want something. My mom, for example, she wanted her nipples to stop hurting. Frankie at age six was a suckling machine! But that's why I mostly sleep with whores these days. Sure, they want something too, but they're up-front about it. I'm a big fan of honesty (in others). Anyway, I hope you can learn something from my mistakes. Some of the women I've banged were a lot of fun, but at the end of the day, nothing beats a great whore. As my friend Charlie Sheen once said, "I don't pay them to have sex with me, I pay them to leave." These days I strive for forgettability in my sex life. And I forget most everyone I banged, so here's a list of ten: Some I banged, some I didn't, some I'm not sure. So here, enjoy, God bless . . .

1. Eleanor Roosevelt

I probably have her on a pedestal because she was my first crush. I went to Eleanor Roosevelt Middle School and every morning I was greeted by her horse-faced mug. There's something about a lady with a set of choppers and I bet she knew how to use them. I still get a little chub going when I see an old lady wearing a fancy hat. The things she could have taught me . . . heard she swung both ways too. That is good. That is always good. Unless she's a stud. And Eleanor was all filly, not at the end, but at some point. Anyways, I digress. You get the point.

2. Suzy Kolber

Joe Namath had the right idea when he tried to kiss this saucy little number on *Monday Night Football*. Then the next thing you know they're sending Broadway Joe away to rehab. Just for trying to swap spit with the hottest sportsbabe since Phyllis George? Talk about illegal procedure.

3. Squeaky Fromme

Well I have a good guess as to why they call her Squeaky, that's for damn sure. She was so loud in the sack I needed earplugs half the time. Small price to pay for that piece of ass, though. I got into some weird shit in the sixties, and I was always drawn to the batshit broads. You can say a lot of things about Charlie Manson, but you cannot say that the man didn't know how to party. He was a hell of a lot more fun than those Beach Boys pussies. My only regret is that my last conversation with Squeaks was a fight. She was yelling about bad vibes coming from the TV whenever the news was on and I told her to put a sock in it and that if she had something to say about it she should say it to the president. She grabbed my gun and walked out. I never saw her again, and that's a shame. Good kid.

4. Anna Mae Bullock

Sure, you may know her as Tina Turner, but I can't bring myself to say that name. For me she'll always be Anna Mae, that sweet, shy girl I had the pleasure of meeting in '67. (I was really all over the place in the '60s.) Club Manhattan was jumping that December 24 and there she was, sitting with her sister at a table. One look and I was dreaming of a brown Christmas, if you know what I'm saying. Anyway I pulled the old "spill a drink on the pretty lady, then offer to buy yourself a replacement" trick and it worked like a charm. Soon I was dabbing whiskey off her boobs and she was dragging me out back.

Whoa, man, I will never forget the two and a half minutes that followed. I had four orgasms and was headed for a fifth when from behind me I heard, "Motherfucker best not have his dick in my Anna Mae." I quickly removed said dick, hoping no one would be the wiser, but that Ike was one canny dude. I knew I was taking my life in my hands, but I told him straight up that love was love, and who was he, and who was I, to deny it. I said that Anna Mae and I were headed out of town and not letting anything stand in our way, not even death itself. I even let it slip that my mother's name was Tina. Ike got real quiet, then he turned to Anna Mae and said, "Tina, you come with me. We ain't got time for this white man and his Oedipussy shit. You hear me?" She just said, "Yes, Daddy," and followed him back into the club. Ike was just another prick trying to label me as a nitwit, but fuck Tina for leaving. I realize, in retrospect, that I just had a soft spot for Nubian princesses with pipes.

5. Billie Jean King

Sure, you know her as the sexiest athlete of the seventies, but I knew a shy, awkward naif who was just learning about the world and the pleasures of her womanly body. She was a big fan of pillow talk. I'm not usually one for it but she got me going on and on about Eleanor Roosevelt—she was a bit of an Ellie historian herself. After our brief fling she said that I "taught her a lot about men" and that she would be making some major changes because of it. Nothing like a good porking to get a woman's head straight, am I right?

6. Christine McVie

Okay, listen. This is the last time I'm going to say this. I am NOT responsible for Fleetwood Mac breaking up. All the drama aside, Christie was something special. But as usual I screwed it up. You know that song "Little Lies"? That one's about me. I told her I was six foot two. Goddamn Stevie ratted me out. Stupid, Frank. Stupid stupid stupid.

7. Miley Cyrus

I came in like a wrecking ball, if you know what I'm saying.

8. Shaun Cassidy

Okay, I wrote a little something about a chick I remembered being super sexy from the early eighties. Then I had someone look her up on them gadgets and realized it was a dude. Who spells it Shaun? Shaun's a chick's name! Disregard this one, moving on.

9. Snooki

Hey, if she has a rum ham, I'm in, baby. Who turns down rum ham?

10. Jackie Kennedy

Queen of Camelot . . . I know I was still a young pup when her old man got taken out by the commies, but I thought I might one day have a shot. What a time that would have been, what a time. Anyway, she ended up marrying some rich prick. I dodged a bullet there. Everyone who put a ring on that broad ended up in a casket.

7

Devotion

By Charlie (as told to Frank)

It's Frank again. I came home the other day and found Charlie trying to write something, but he was having some trouble. So I offered to help him out. He'd gotten as far as this:

Meny lady not realize what mess lyfe bi withow Charlie. Charlie gud man. Charlie sterng man. Charlie wochbadstoccer. Charlie protect so gud all day. Charlie always there be no matter what jutj say. No matter stainer order say. Charlie so gud love so sterng love so much love sumtime.

What he's trying to say is that love knows no bounds. It's a force of nature and can't be contained, certainly not by something as puny as a restraining order. He goes on to list the things a man should do for the woman he loves. In the interest of legibility I had him dictate them to me. He may not be much in the writing department, but I've never seen a man who understands women better.

THINGS A MAN SHOULD DO FOR

THE WOMAN HE LOVES

➡ **Be forgiving.** Forgive her for sleeping with your roommate. Forgive her for sleeping with your best friend. Forgive her for sleeping with your other best friend. Forgive her for sleeping with Schmitty. Forgive her for having you arrested.

➡ **Pay attention to the little things.** Like the squiggly things you see when you put her saliva under a microscope.

➡ **Give her a back rub using her favorite lotion or skin cream.** Don't press too hard, though, or you'll wake her.

➡ **Do her laundry, but don't make a big deal out of it.** In fact, don't even tell her you did it. Or that you were in her apartment while she was at work. Do NOT tell her you kept any of her laundry.

➡ **Remember birthdays and anniversaries.** Send her a card on Mac's, Dee's, Dennis's, and Frank's birthdays too. Send her five cards on your birthday. Send cards on the anniversaries of the day you fixed her plumbing, your whirlwind romance at the Jersey Shore, and the first day she turned you down for a date. She'll be touched that you remembered the good times.

➡ **If she's an alcoholic, become one too.** Then you can go through recovery together. Watch that thirteenth step, it's a doozy!

➡ **If she returns your letters unopened, you can easily get her a note by attaching it to a brick and lobbing it into her living room.** There's no such thing as an unopened brick!

➠ **Write and stage a musical.** It is literally the most romantic thing in the world. Everyone will want to marry you, but only marry her!

➠ **Date other women to make her burn with jealous rage.** If that doesn't work, put cayenne in her underwear to make her burn with jealous rage. Remember, when she yells at you about it, it's just because she's jealous. She's so cute when she's jealous.

➠ **Keep an eye on the bad stalker.** *

➠ **Impress her with your compassion by pretending to be a Big Brother to some punk kid.**

➠ **Distract her from work stress.** One good way is to tell her you have cancer.

➠ **Want to see her in a pinch?** List her as your emergency contact, then get in a terrible car accident.

➠ **Find and destroy the video your best friend secretly made of him having sex with her.** Try not to watch it first.

➠ **Find and destroy the copies you made of the video of your best friend having sex with her.** Try not to watch them first. (Keep one copy just in case.)

➠ **Encourage her dreams.** The best way to understand her dreams is to go into her apartment at night and watch her sleep. Be careful not to step on her cat.

➠ **Send her a gift basket filled with erotic cheeses on her birthday and holidays.**

➠ **Spend fifteen minutes when she gets home from work talking about her day.** If you talk loud enough she'll hear you, even though you're standing alone outside her building.

➠ **Want to attend that dinner party you weren't invited to?** Sew yourself into her couch!†

---

* FRANK: When I asked Charlie who the "bad stalker" was he got cagey and just kept repeating, "You just gotta keep an eye on him no matter what you just gotta keep an eye on him."

† FRANK: He learned this one from me. Glad to see I'm rubbing off on the kid.

➡ **Pick a dandelion from the sidewalk and put it in her hair.** Use Krazy Glue, so it lasts.

➡ **Write a love poem and leave it on her pillow.** Do NOT write it in your own blood. Rat blood dries faster and most people can't tell the difference.

➡ **Above all, just always be there for her.** All the time. No matter how many times she begs you to go or threatens to have you arrested or pays people to break your legs. That's just her way of testing you. Don't waver. Because if you really truly love someone, you'll never leave them alone. Never. Ever. Ever. Ever. Ever. Ever.*

---

* FRANK: I only included the first five "ever"s here; Charlie said a whole lot more.

I Beat Marriage
and So Can You

By Dennis

It may surprise you to hear this coming from someone so youthful and robust, but I was married once, to my high school sweetheart. A swell gal named Maureen. Sadly, our union was not destined to last forever,[*] but looking back on it now I can honestly say that I walked away from the experience having learned some extremely valuable life lessons.

When considering marriage, the first thing you need to do is create a proper framework for thinking about whether or not you should actually do it. The first question you have to ask yourself is "Am I totally high on crack?" If the answer is no, then the next question you should ask yourself is "Why, if I'm not totally high on crack, am I even thinking about getting married?" Chances are the answer to this is either that you're being desperate or that you're being mature. Be very careful when answering this question. The two reasons are only separated by a very, very fine line. Many desperate losers have wrapped themselves in a self-deluded mantle of maturity, trying to convince themselves that they aren't sad or lonely and that they don't look like a giant bird. Around here we call it DRS.[†] I've found that when trying to sort through the uncertainty surrounding these issues, a few moments of quiet meditation can be extremely helpful. If that doesn't do the trick, I'll smoke a teeny tiny rock of crack.[‡]

If you've come to the conclusion you're being mature in your decision to get married, the best advice I can give you is to go pound off right now. I'm dead serious. Right now. And don't bring me to the bathroom with you either. I'll wait here, thank you very much. Okay, you back? Great. Go do it again. I don't care if your dick is tired; this is important. Before you answer the next question I have for you, you need to have pounded off twice in quick succession.

Okay, all done? Good. Now pull out a picture of your "beloved" and take a long look. Now take a long look inside your soul. Finally, take a long look inside your penis. Now, here's the question you need to answer: Do you still feel like getting married or would you rather be

---

[*] Or, indeed, even forty-eight hours.

[†] Dee Reynolds Syndrome.

[‡] The trick is to just smoke enough that you feel AMAZING, but not so much that you start making bad decisions.

napping? Napping sounds pretty good right about now, huh? I'll tell you, I got sick of Maureen Ponderosa in only a day or so, but I've never been sick of napping. In fact, I know napping and I will be friends for life. Guess what? I just saved you from a shitload of heartache and attorneys' fees. Feel free to send me a check, care of Paddy's Pub.

Now, I know what you're thinking: "But, Dennis, what if earlier on I came to the conclusion that I was desperate, not mature?" Well, my friend, that's an entirely different situation. If you truly are desperate, then this might be your one shot at finding someone to clean your apartment and make the bed and do your laundry and cook your meals and put her pinkie up your butt while she blows you.[*] You need to think long and hard about this, friend,[†] because it's possible the lone-wolf lifestyle is not for you. You know those schlumpy TV sitcom husbands who are fat and hate their wives, but somehow they just stay together forever because it would screw up the show if they actually acted in their own self-interest? That might be you! Don't fight your true nature. If you really are a purposeless sack of protoplasm who's just sitting around eating your wife's meatloaf[‡] while watching reruns of *The Honeymooners* or whatever other crap is on Nick at Nite, and waiting for your heart to give out, then crap, you need to get married *yesterday*.

But before you pull the trigger and take the plunge and tie the knot and slaughter the calf and take the long walk off the short pier and settle for the bird in the hand when you could be banging all the sweet-ass doves in that bush over there, I do have some advice about what happens after the honeymoon.[§]

The toughest thing about making marriage work over the long haul is not getting sick of each other. After I married Maureen, I came to real-

---

[*] Just the pinkie. Anything larger gauge than the pinkie is gay.[**]

   [**] Even if the word "pinkie" is actually the gayest thing in the universe.

[†] And not just about whether she washed her hands before she made you dinner.

[‡] Did she wash her hands? Are you *sure*?

[§] For advice on what happens during the honeymoon, please see my other book, *Sex Secrets: The Golden God Tells All*.

ize that those little quirks and peccadilloes that were so cute during the honeymoon phase were deal-breakers in the long run, like her calling me "babe" all the time and wearing ugly sweaters with cats on them and having a disgusting dead tooth. This is where your choice of mate becomes critical. They either need to (a) have no discernible personality whatsoever, thereby giving you nothing to get sick of, or (b) be weak-willed enough that you can, through subtle behavior-modification protocols, mold them into whatever acceptable set of behaviors you deem appropriate for your household.

Say she starts getting all jealous and bent out of shape simply because you refuse to throw out an expansive collection of sex tapes you've spent years compiling. This is a simple matter of recontextualizing the situation. She's not really asking her man to give up his passion, is she? His art? His *life's work*, for god's sake? It's a good thing you had this talk now because you're glad to know she's the kind of rude, selfish whore of a woman who would ever do something like that to the kind, generous, caring man in her life. If she doesn't go for this, then you've got someone with entirely too much personality on your hands.

The final thing you need to ensure the perfect marriage is to figure out your stance on cheating. Now and again you'll run into people who get very judgmental on this topic. Do not be swayed by their high-and-mighty BS. Only *you* can know if cheating is right for you. And there's only one way to find out. Get out there and cheat, even if you don't feel like it.

When I was at Penn, I attended a lecture by a renowned sociologist named Eric Anderson who calls monogamy a "socially compelled sexual incarceration" that can lead to a life of anger and contempt. That filled me with inspiration.* Finally someone was knocking down the Big Lie upon which the institution of marriage was built. Men have penises and they need to put them in ladies. Not lady. Men putting their penises in

---

* And made me tumescent. A "brain boner" if you will.

lady just doesn't sound right. And if there's one thing I know, if it don't sound right, it ain't right.

So get out there and bang a few people and see if you like it.* If you don't like it, don't judge yourself too harshly. You might just be really boring. If it's not for you, relax. Your life is actually simpler. All the trouble is over now. Settle in. Maybe invest in a La-Z-Boy. You've got a good forty years of meatloaf ahead of you† and some truly fantastic TV to watch. That Dobie Gillis is a hoot, isn't he?

* There is a VERY good chance you will like it.
† Protip: Set up your La-Z-Boy with a view to the kitchen sink, so you can make sure she's washing her hands.

9

Here's How

Straight I Am

By Mac

L et's get one thing about me "straight" up-front. When it comes to sexuality, I'm about as hetero as they come. If a gay guy came on to me, I'd be like, "No way, bro. I'm a straight-up party boy who's into chicks." Yup, one gay dude wouldn't stand a chance. It would take at least four or five gay guys strapping me down to make it inside me. Sorry, fellas, that's just how straight I am.

And even then I wouldn't make it easy. I'd be like, "Hey look! There goes George Michael!" And they'd all shriek "Where?!" at once, and I'd make a break for it, and they'd be like, "He's getting away! Chase him! I want his butt!" But I wouldn't just give them my butt. They'd have to take it. And once they got me strapped down, I'd stop fighting it because that would be giving them what they want. And I don't want them to enjoy it. If anyone's going to enjoy it, it's going to be me. So, I'd just relax into it and taunt them by telling them how ripped and sexy I find them and letting them know how much I'm enjoying myself. So, even though I'd have a bunch of ripped guys all taking turns on my butt, I'd still be enjoying it. But only because I forced myself to. It's not like I could fight these guys off. There are too many of them and they want me too much. What am I, Chuck Norris?*

I'm not against homosexuality, though. I say to each his own. You're free to do whatever you want. But you shouldn't be able to get married, because marriage is sacred. And if gays are able to get married, then what's next? People marrying watermelons? However, this is a free country and you should have all the same rights as us straight people, except for certain rights that you shouldn't have because you're gay. And even though God has a plan for you and He made you the way you are, he's sending you to hell, because you also had free will. Okay, Dennis just told me that last part doesn't make sense so I had to explain to him that that's where faith plays into all this. Now, I don't have time to explain why faith trumps facts right now, so why don't you go ahead and pull out the big book and have God explain that one Himself. In conclusion, just always remember that even though God is sending you to hell, He loves you and He always will.

---

* I know, gay guys, this is a shock. But I'm actually not.

You Gotta Have

a Sidekick

By Frank

There are only three worthwhile things that sonofabitch father of mine ever taught me. The first is that hoagies taste best when you make them in your mouth. The secret is swigging a little olive oil after you put in the meat and cheese but before you stuff in the bread and peppers. And okay, fine, my brother, Gino, actually taught me that, but our pops showed it to him first, so it counts. And Gino's a prick, so I'll tell you when he'll be getting credit for anything from me—never, that's when!

But the other thing—and this one my father taught me directly—is that if you wanna get by in this life, you better get yourself a good sidekick.

"Frank," he'd always say, "it's a dog-eat-dog world out there, and two dogs got twice the bite as one. They also take twice as many dumps, which comes in handy when shit starts going down." I never understood that last part. I asked my old man about it once when I was twelve and he explained it to me the best way he knew how, by whacking me upside the head with one of his shoes. After that I didn't ask him many questions, especially not when he was wearing those Florsheim wing tips with the wooden heels my ma got him for Christmas. Bitch.

When I was growing up, my brother, Gino, was my main sidekick. We were like two peas in a pod, me and Gino. We did everything together—from banging broads to singing in a doo-wop group to doing giant mountains of cocaine, sometimes all three in the same night. If it weren't for Shadynasty we'd probably be pals to this day. I won't get into it here though, except to say that everything that went down was Gino's fault.

I've had a few other sidekicks since Gino tried to cuckold me. I'll never forget Bao Nguyen, one of my 'Nam buddies. You never saw a better tailor. If it hadn't been for that fire, I was going to move him up to foreman. Guy would have been paid in actual cash! Dumb bastard. Everyone knows sweatshops don't have smoke alarms.

Once I got back stateside there was Eugene Hamilton. We started ReyHam Properties together and built it into a multimillion-dollar business. Unfortunately we were forced to split up once the money was too good for me not to steal it all. Way to ruin the magic, Eugene.

What I'm trying to say is that I've been around a long time and that means I've had a lot of sidekicks. And I've made a lot of mistakes with those sidekicks. I want to spare you the same fate. For instance, you shouldn't ever start an insurance fire if Bao is still in the factory. It's a surefire way to lose a friend. (Get it? Sure*fire*? Still got it, Frankie.) But the most important thing is how to pick the right sidekick in the first place. You don't want to end up with a schmuck like Eugene who makes so much money you're forced to dick him over.

The first thing you look for in a sidekick is loyalty. You need to know you can trust the guy to have your back no matter how much you lie to him. Another key thing is street smarts. That's what's so great about Charlie—he knows all the good Dumpsters and can kill a rat with anything. Seriously! Plus we've been sleeping together for the better part of ten years, and I just don't share my pull-out couch with anybody. Well, I do, but I don't sleep in it with just anybody. Charlie's got "it" when it comes to being a good sidekick. Love that kid.

The third thing you want in a sidekick is speed, and I don't mean drugs (though that's a big plus). You want to know if he can run. If he can, keep clear! That prick'll get you killed. Remember the law of the jungle: you don't have to be faster than the lion, just faster than the guy you're with. For a guy his age, Charlie's slow as shit, which is just my speed.

Finally, you need a good nickname for you and your buddy. Charlie and I are the Gruesome Twosome. One of the main reasons people don't mess with us is that name. And the fact that I wave guns around a lot. Mac and Dennis call themselves the Dynamic Duo, which they stole from some Korean rap group I think. Pretty unoriginal, if you ask me, but they always were amateur hour as far as I'm concerned. And Dee, wait, let's see, who was Dee's . . . Geez, you know what? I just realized. Dee doesn't have a sidekick! She's a lonely spinster who doesn't have a sidekick or a nickname to go with her sad, lonely life.

Which brings me to the third thing my dad used to tell me all the time: "No matter how hard you try, no matter how much you whack them up the side of their heads with your wing tips, kids always grow up to be disappointments." Wise old sonofabitch, my old man.

11

A Man and His Horse: The Story of Peter Nincompoop

By Charlie (as told to Dennis)

Friends come in all shapes and sizes. Mostly they're people-sized, but not always. Sometimes friends are shaped like other things. Like a bird with teeth, or a jar of glue, or a block of cheddar. They can be horse-shaped too, like my awesome friend Peter Nincompoop. She was shaped like a white horse, because a white horse is what she was. Or is. To be honest, I'm not sure if Peter Nincompoop is even still alive anymore.

Last time I saw her, she took off running down the alley behind Paddy's. And while the streets of Philadelphia are awesome for lots of things, they're probably not so great for horses running wild. People in Philly have guns, and many of them are angry (the people and the guns). I worry because, well, they shoot horses, don't they? Still, I hope Peter Nincompoop is alive, because as friends go, she's one of the most loyal and easy to talk to and ride around on that I've ever had.

Peter Nincompoop would never do anything to make a friend feel uncomfortable . . . well, except for that time she kicked the stable boy's brains in. My guess is that she and the stable boy probably weren't friends to begin with, though. There's no way in hell they had the sort of connection me and Peter Nincompoop had. It's weird, she would look at me, and I would look at her, and it was like we were one and the same. Like we were a horse-person. I think, maybe, I was a centaur in my past life.

I love you, Peter Nincompoop.

QUIZ
QUORNER

By Dee

Hey, Sweet Dee here. I don't know about you turkeys, but I've had enough of crappy relationships. I'm ready for the *quality*, people. So before we get rolling with this thing I figured it couldn't hurt to just let you know that I'm available if any of you happen to be hot single rich guys who don't smoke or have kids and are interested in embarking upon a mind-blowing sexual odyssey with a statuesque blonde (who's at least a nine, maybe a ten) in exchange for regular financial support. (That's a nine or ten in hotness, by the way, not dress size. If you must know, I'm a petite four.)

Actually, if you're really rich, you don't even have to be single. We can fix that. And you know what? I'm going to go ahead and say smoking's okay too, as long as it's not that clove shit. Clove cigarettes are for chicks in bands that play Lilith Fair and unemployed artists who are too white to smoke. Nah, you're too rich for that, aren't you? But you're wounded because you're only sort of hot and the money hasn't been the consolation you thought it would be. I get it. Listen, I don't want to put my e-mail in this book for all the schlubs out there to see, but if you're interested, get in touch with Damon, our new editor at Titan Books. It's damon@titan-books.com. Shoot him a recent bank statement and I'll be in touch if the whole "us" thing makes sense.

Now, before the rest of you go judging me, I don't just have sex with rich guys. But the more cash you have, the easier it is for me to see your inner beauty. I know, it's weird, but it works. For example, I would have sex with the starting catcher for the Phillies. Sure, he's short and Mexican or Colombian or something, and he's got some weird acne going on, but I read in the paper this morning that he just signed a five-year deal worth $50 million. And as the song says, that kind of bling buys lots of pinkie rings.

I *would not*, on the other hand, have sex with the backup catcher for the Phillies. I don't even know who it is, but he's a backup. On a team that didn't even make the play-offs. And catchers are usually fat and boring. And I seriously meant the part about no kids. That's nonnegotiable. Ew!

Anyway, when I said I'm over relationships, what I really meant was I'm over this section of the book. It's only the first one and I'm already bored as shit with being an author. I don't get how people have the time or patience to write these things, especially knowing that no one reads anymore. The only reason I'm even bothering with this writing bullshit is that the guys said we have to turn in fifty thousand words in order to get the rest of our advance. And since the catcher for the Phillies hasn't called yet, Momma needs her cabbage.

But even though books suck, you know what people still *do* read? Awesome magazine quizzes like the ones in *Cosmo*.

They're fun, and they take up a *lot* of space. That's why I suggested we put a quiz in this book—to put a dent in that stupid word count. Plus you can just copy quiz questions straight out of the magazines. Like I did here. All those things sound the same anyway. No one'll know the difference.

Still, the guys said the answers on the old quizzes were retarded and for once I agree with those jerks, so we made up some different answers and called it a day. My work is done. And so, thank Christ, is this section.

WHAT'S YOUR RELATIONSHIP IQ?

One of the most important aspects of maintaining a successful relationship is understanding what makes relationships work in the first place. So, you think you know a lot about relationships? Take the quiz and find out.

1. Whenever you pass a bridal magazine on a newsstand you . . .

   ❏   a. roll your eyes. All those beaming chicks in white dresses look like Stepford wives.

   ❏   b. stop, smile, and think, "Gee, someday that could be me. If my cans come in and/ or I can find someone to love me the way I am."

   ❏   c. stop, smile, and think, "Gee, I would totally bang the shit out of that chick. I've never seen a black chick in a wedding

dress. I like the color contrast. Wow, I
really need black friends."
- ❏   d. thumb through it and wonder how a
goddamn cake could possibly cost more
than $20, much less upward of $20,000.

2. On a TV titillation scale, sex with the same person for the
rest of your life is like . . .
- ❏   a. reruns. You can only do it so many times
before it gets predictable.
- ❏   b. a long romantic epic. Carnal classics
never grow stale with the perfect costar.
- ❏   c. a documentary about assisted suicide.
- ❏   d. Wait, what? There are TVs that have tits?
I'll take two.

3. What's your top priority when you're at a club?
- ❏   a. Mooching off other people's bottle
service.
- ❏   b. Dancing (i.e., prebanging).
- ❏   c. Seeing if they serve cheese.
- ❏   d. Convincing chicks we don't know
Charlie.

4. Do you ever fantasize about one of your exes being "the
one that got away"?
- ❏   a. I've wondered "What if?" but it passes.
- ❏   b. I could get any of my exes back with a
come-hither look.
- ❏   c. That's what the sex tape drawer is for.

❑   d. Do trannies count?

❑   e. If by "ex" you mean "someone I had
chained up in Paddy's basement for a
year," then yes. Every day.

5. What do your friends and family think of your partner?

❑   a. Partner?

❑   b. Are you calling me gay?

❑   c. They don't know that *she* ever had one,
so it'd be fine since she's technically a girl
anyway.

6. Do you believe in love at first sight?

❑   a. That is a childish notion. I'm an adult for
god's sake. Wanna bang?

❑   b. I believe in hug at first sight. And that it
shouldn't be an arrestable offense.

❑   c. I believe in shove at first sight, but only
with dudes.

❑   d. I believe when a giant bird and a man
love each other very much, something
magical happens. That magical thing is
the man leaving and Dee being alone
forever.

7. Picture your partner being with someone else. What emotion do you feel the most?

❑   a. Jealousy.

❑   b. Anger.

   ❏   c. Sadness.

   ❏   d. A boner.

   ❏   e. Threesome.

   ❏   f. "Why did I introduce her to Dennis?"

8. When you talk to your partner, who starts the conversations?

   ❏   a. Me.

   ❏   b. Him.

   ❏   c. Her.

   ❏   d. It.

   ❏   e. I give her my money, she raises the bar on the tollbooth. It's beyond words.

9. The first thing you look for in a potential partner is . . .

   ❏   a. honesty and a sense of humor.

   ❏   b. signs of an STD.

   ❏   c. ginormous cans.

   ❏   d. potential exits.

10. The statement "I can usually intuit what other people are feeling" is . . .

   ❏   a. not at all true.

   ❏   b. somewhat true.

   ❏   c. mostly true.

   ❏   d. very true.

   ❏   e. Let's drop the game. It's okay that you want to have sex with me. Very common reaction.

11. You and your partner are taking a walk in the park. One of you spots a fifty-dollar bill fall out of an elderly lady's purse. After discussing this situation, what do you and your partner do?

☐ a. Go see *Thunder Gun Express 2: The Rectification* in 3-D. Large popcorn for me. Water for fatty.

☐ b. Explain that we are her long-lost grandchildren. And that we are so, so hungry.

☐ c. We take the money and go buy the old lady a bottle of whiskey. On our return, when we are unable to locate her, we drink the booze in her honor.

☐ d. Snatch her purse. Otherwise, she's just gonna keep walking around like an idiot, dropping money all over the park, until someone mugs her.

12. You are friends with another couple. You know that one of the people in that couple had an affair. Do you tell the spouse about it?

☐ a. Yes.

☐ b. No.

☐ c. Only if it slips out accidentally.

☐ d. Depends. Is the female member of this couple attractive? If so, would my revealing her spouse's indiscretion potentially lead to the two of us having revenge sex? If so, definitely. However, if the attractive female member of the couple is the cheater, blackmail is a more effective way to resolve the situation, where I get to bang that dirty little two-timing sex kitten up-front, then extort her secret for cold hard cash (and the occasional BJ on the side) for years to come.

13. The holidays are coming up. How do you decide which family to spend the holiday with—yours or your partner's?

❏   a. Theirs.
❏   b. Theirs.
❏   c. Theirs.
❏   d. Paddy's.

Answer key:
Give yourself 5 points for every "a" answer. Each "b" answer is worth 9 points. A "c" is totally worthless—in fact, if you answered "c" to any of these questions, give yourself a –50 and accept that you are going to be alone for the rest of your life. "D," on the other hand, is like a golden ticket. If you answered "d" one or more times, you win forever. At everything. The "e"s and "f"s are worth a point each, unless you answered "e" and "f" together. In which case you're a total jabroni. Take your final score, subtract 10, multiply by 16.3, and punch yourself in the face as hard as you can.

PART II

Financial Success and Career

The Bone-Crushing

Power of Words

By Mac

I t's amazing how many words there are in the English language that I don't know. Or, I should say, *didn't* know. Ever since we started writing the most awesome magnum opus in the universe, I've taken it upon myself to memorize *at least* one new word every week. (See how focused I am on my new career as an author? I'm doing this for you AND for me.) I also took it upon myself to learn how to *italicize* words that are *especially* important. It's easy. Highlight the word, then press the "command" and "I" keys at the same time. *Like this.* Frank's always going around saying, "You can't teach an old dog new tricks," but I guess I'm proving that asshole wrong again. Pretty **bold** of me, huh? I think I've uncovered the <u>underlining</u> problem with that type of thinking. Anyone who thinks this dog is done picking up new tricks can ~~go fuck himself~~ go to hell. I could do this all day if I wanted to. But that's a big if.

This week I went ahead and learned three new words: "magnum opus," "*italicize*" (always *italicize* the word "*italicize*"), and "pantheon." Actually, come to think of it, that's *four* words, since "magnum" and "opus" are separate words that when put together mean one word: "masterpiece." Holy shit, did you see what I just did there, connecting seemingly random words with the seemingly correct definition? It just came to me, not on purpose, but, like, out of thin air. It's seriously goddamn crazy how smart I'm getting ever since I became an author. If I keep this up, pretty soon my brain itself will be a magnum opus. A magnum opus of learned stuff. I'll be like the guy in *Rain Man*, only with a smaller nose and way more muscles and my name plastered on the cover of a bestseller. Take that, autistics!

As far as the word "pantheon" goes, I saw it in the newspaper the other day in an article about Chase Utley. It said, "Chase Utley has entered the pantheon of Phillies greats." And I got super pissed because to me it sounded like the dude that wrote it was throwing shade on the most awesome player in Phillies history. I mean let's be serious, "pantheon" sounds a lot like the words "pansy" and "tampon" banged each other and nine months later they gave birth to a weird little deformed thing called a pantheon. Ew. And given that the Phillies wear form-fitting white-and-red uniforms, well, you can easily see how I could assume something like that. Reminds me of a similar thing that happened a couple of years ago when the Channel 6 sports guy referred to Donovan McNabb as "colorful" and I was like, Bro, easy on the goddamn racism, bro. The fact that the Channel 6 sports guy is also black doesn't help either. That's what's known as "reverse racism." Look it up. It happens all the time.

Anyways, I was so PO'd about Chase getting called a pantheon by this reporter jabroni that I was about to head down to the *Daily News* to hammer the shit out of the guy. And then I stopped. And I realized something important. Any knucklehead can go hammer a guy without really understanding why he's hammering him. But now that I'm an author, I've also become a thinker, and what does a thinker do? He *thinks* about his actions before he *actions* them. So instead of actioning up some action, I actioned up some thinking. I thought about *why* I felt like crushing every bone in that sportswriter's face. And the answer was simple: He called Chase a pantheon. So I looked it up. Turns out "pantheon" means "the place of the heroes or idols of any group, individual, movement, party, etc."

That dickhead reporter wasn't slamming Chase at all! He was calling him a hero. And you know what? By not straight-up wrecking that dude no questions asked, *I* became a hero myself. A book-writing, word-looking-upping, newspaper-reading hero. One who's ready to enter the pantheon hand in hand with Mr. Chase Utley . . . and, believe me, <u>there</u> are no *words* to describe how **badass** that's going to be.

Conflict Resolution

By Dennis

H ey, guys, let's have a little informal rap session here. We're gonna get real for a sec, so let it all hang out. If you ask me, it's really the only way to solve anything. Get in there and *work it out* for reals. If you couldn't tell by my tone, I'm sitting backward in a chair *and* I'm wearing a baseball cap backward. That's just how real this rap session is going to get.

Because today we're going to talk about the C-word, guys. That's right.

Conflict.

Some say conflict is the root of all conflict in the world and I say those people are right. But you know what I also say? I say we get *rid* of conflict and have world peace instead.

Okay, did you see what I did there?* See, I'll bet you didn't even notice. I better slow it down. There are ways to use precisely calibrated language to squash beefs before they even start. In the previous para-

---

* Besides put myself in line for a Nobel Peace Prize.

graph, I used what psychologists call an "I Message." I Messages start with "I" and are used to put the person you're talking to at ease by taking the pressure off them. "You Messages," on the other hand, start with "you" and sound accusatory and aggressive. They put people on the defensive. You've probably used You Messages tons of times without thinking about it. But not anymore. Today's the day you stop being an inconsiderate monster everyone secretly hates.

Next time you feel like saying something, before you open your yap and make a fool out of yourself and everyone who loves you, reformulate your statement as an I Message. Once you do that simple trick, it pretty much becomes illegal for the other person to get mad at you. Here's an example: *I* get uncomfortable when *you* act like an idiot and use You Messages.

See how that works? Even someone of your limited intelligence could figure it out. Let's workshop a little.

How can we turn around the sentence "*You* are far less attractive than I am, therefore you should get off the stage"? It's really quite simple; I'd just say: "*I* can't believe I actually paid money to see this shit."*

Think you got it? Okay, hotshot, take a crack at fixing this one: "*Your* failure to recognize my superior cheekbones is deeply distressing to everyone here." Simple. Put an "I" up front and say: "*I* think we all know who the asshole is."†

And hey, listen, I'm not perfect.‡ Just the other day, for instance, I saw Dee counting out her tips after her shift and my first instinct was to say, "*You* look just like a giant ugly bird." But I didn't. Because I remembered I'm not a conflict-driven person and I don't want to stir anyone up. So instead I simply said, "*I* wonder who left this big smelly bird in here. Oh wait, that's not a bird, it's Dee! Hi, Dee!"

---

* Make sure you shout it loud enough to be heard in a noisy music venue. Remember, self-improvement never takes a day off.

† For the record, the asshole is the person who refuses to acknowledge my cheekbones.

‡ Though I understand how you'd make that mistake.

I remember that time we all went to see a shrink and Mac said: "*You* leave this pen here and people are supposed to think, 'Wait, that looks like a dick.'" See, there's a guy who's just asking for conflict. Convert that into the appropriate I Message and it goes like this: "*I* secretly want to bang dudes."

And that's it. Pretty simple stuff, but you'd be amazed how powerful it can be. Look, I'm not saying I just changed the world for the better,[*] but I think I kind of just changed the world for the better.[†] Does that make me better than most people? It's not for me to say. I didn't choose to be the harbinger of a new era of peace and understanding, just like I didn't choose to be a golden god walking among mortals, teaching them the ways of the Fair Ones. You just have to take life as it comes.

And on that note, I'd like to send one more I Message to our publisher. Hey, Titan Books, *I* would appreciate it if *you* guys could start sending some perks our way.[‡] *I*'m about to be a bestselling author, which means not only do *I* have a toxically excessive lifestyle to get used to, *you* are about to owe us your very livelihood. It would be a shame if we were to get *conflict*ed about who we let publish this little masterpiece, wouldn't it?

---

[*] Yet.

[†] There it is.

[‡] Limos, a six-figure wardrobe budget, and a couple ounces of blow would be a good place to start.

Getting

Rich off

Your Kids

By Frank

All my life I've been able to make pretty good money. I don't know why, I just have a head for business and stuff like that. But if I could've figured out a way to get rich off one of my kids instead of having to do it off the sweat of my own hump, you bet your ass I would have been all over that like wart scars on my dong.

Now, if you do manage to get some good dollars coming your way just because your kid turns out to be a whiz at computers or acting or robbing banks, you can count on some bleeding-heart liberal coming at you. You know—all that whiny bullshit about how you "shouldn't endanger a child's welfare" or "steal their childhood" or "teach them to use automatic weapons." Take it from me, these people are misinformed about the positive effects of hard work on a kid.

Hell, for every bad seed like that Linda Lohan there's at least ten Shirley Temples and Judy Garlands. There are tons of people who start out working hard (and making tall dollars for the real heroes, their parents) and then go on to lead perfectly normal well-adjusted lives. If you got a kid who's showing talent at an early age at singing or begging or sing-begging,* you owe it to yourself and to this country to ride the little brat all the way to the bank. This is America and we have the right to do whatever the hell we want to our kids. That's what makes this country great.

Okay, I just went back and reread that last part, and realized I need to clarify something. What I meant to say was we can do *almost* whatever the hell we want with our kids. There is one rule you HAVE to follow, or, believe me, there'll be hell to pay.

You can't diddle 'em. Not your own kids or anyone else's. Hell, you can't even let people get the idea you'd want to. I certainly don't want to. I don't! Hell, I spent twenty years married to someone who was the furthest thing from a kid. That's proof isn't it? God, she was an old bat. But I still banged her and pretended I liked it. And not once while I was in there was I thinking about a kid. I might have been thinking about how much I hoped I wouldn't knock the bitch up and *have* a kid.[†] But I screwed that up enough times that I eventually stopped worrying about it and started figuring out ways to make money off 'em.

But it's a simple rule: Money good, diddling bad. You can get rich off 'em all day, so long as no one thinks you're up to no good when night falls. And here's where it gets really unfair. You have to leave some stuff alone, even though it's 100 percent legit. Like child beauty pageants. Sure, it's an American tradition to dress little girls up like sex dolls and

---

* Hot tip: Sing-begging is where the tall dollars are at.
† Frankie don't do condoms. That's just the way it is.

parade them around like whores, but listen, no matter how classy and enriching that might sound, I can tell ya from firsthand experience it ain't worth it. Not for a dude anyway. I don't care how much you don't ever ever think about kids in a sexual way; you put yourself around a bunch of six-year-olds in bikinis and tiaras, and they're practically begging for it. Sorry, *you're* practically begging for it. Suspicion, that is.

So there you have it, folks. Pretty simple. Exploit your kids for money and it'll take your mind off not wanting to exploit them for sex. They'll thank you for it later, believe me. If you're having trouble coming up with ideas, you can try some of my go-tos:

⇒ Pickpocket

Pickpocketing is a trade that will serve them their whole lives and there's no better time to learn it than when they're a kid and they can pretend they didn't know better. Make sure you hang around while they're working, so you can pretend to reprimand them if they get caught. And to make sure they aren't skimming the take.

⇒ Dwarf Impersonator

Not everybody can pretend they're a dwarf, but kids are just the right size. You can use this any number of ways. They can work as scabs during dwarf labor disputes. You can make Charlie think he's hallucinating. The possibilities are endless.[*]

⇒ Security System

If you're carrying something "sensitive" in your trunk that you don't want anyone snooping on, just toss a kid in there with 'em along with a shotgun. Someone presses their nose where it don't belong and whammo! They get a barrel up each nostril. Just don't

---

[*] There's technically no money in making Charlie think he's hallucinating, but that shit is worth its weight in gold, so same thing, right?

give the kid any live ammo. There's no bigger pain in the ass than an uppity brat with a loaded shotgun who's been in the trunk of your car all day.

Finally if your kid really does seem worthless, don't fret. There's always the circus. Believe it or not those ethically ambiguous bastards pay top dollar for healthy white kids they can turn into unhealthy white adults, a.k.a. carnies. Just remember, you won't be seeing much of the little tyke except when the circus passes through town. Which, with most kids, is an improvement for both you and them. I mean seriously, what kid doesn't love the circus?

Waddup, bitches? Sweet Dee has another little brain bomb for your eyeholes. We got a new editor over there at swanky Titan Books named Damon, and I gotta say, I like this guy already. He seems to have taken an interest in me. He's been sending me my own personal assignments. Hand-delivered to the bar, I might add. That can't be cheap. If I had to guess, I'd say he's grooming me to eventually take over writing this book entirely. Or maybe he'll let the gang stay on for this one, but he'll have me write the sequel solo. I mean Mac and Dennis just write about how great they are at screwing and fighting. Charlie can hardly put a sentence together and Frank's too busy being a disgusting slime-pig to take the time to write anything.

Which means it's up to Sweet Dee to save the day again. Hey, what's one more day-saving at this point, am I right? At least Damon seems to have his head screwed on about who's the brains of the operation here. If you're reading this, Damon (and I kind of know you are), give me a call sometime. I've got a lot of ideas for stuff we could do,[*] and something tells me your expense account needs a little workout.

Anyway, suckers, Damon showed impeccable judgment here by asking me to fill you in on some of the stuff I've learned in the acting game. He already picked out the chapter title, all I have to do is fill the page with my signature brand of compassion, wisdom, and quiet strength. Watch and learn.

---

[*] Not all of them sexual.

How to Make Millions

as an Actress and Quit

Your Crappy Bar Job

By Dee

P eople who come to Paddy's Pub are often blown away by what a phenomenal waitress I am. Chumps. The truth is, I'm not a great waitress. Hell, I'm not even a mediocre one. In fact, it's entirely possible that I am the worst waitress in Philadelphia, if not the entire Eastern Seaboard. And I'm totally fine with that, because the only thing I hate more than waitressing at Paddy's is the friggin' lowlife degenerates I have to bring beers to day in and day out at that dump.*

---

* Everyone's always going on and on about Mother Teresa, making her out to be some kind of saint. But I'll tell you what, if ol' Mama T were to spend a good solid week getting hit on and puked on and occasionally shit on—yes, with actual shit—by the

"But, Dee," you're no doubt wondering, "how can you possibly be a terrible waitress when your customers think you're amazing, other waitresses are jealous of your skills, and you make an insane amount of tips despite the fact that a significant portion of your clientele is homeless? Even your employers . . . okay, so maybe your employers are a bunch of clueless turkeys who wouldn't recognize greatness if it bit them in the dong, but deep down even those brain-dead losers harbor immense respect for your abilities and professionalism."

And you know what, mystery person I'll never meet who asks really good questions? You're right! On the surface it does seem crazy for a waitress of my caliber to claim to be bad at her job while there is so much compelling evidence to the contrary. But here's the thing: No matter what the newspapers and the honorary plaques and the bathroom graffiti would have you believe, I *am* a shitty waitress. I just happen to be an *incredible* actress. And for the past ten years I've been giving one of the great performances in modern theater every damn night of the year. I've been *acting* like a great waitress when in fact I'm nothing of the sort. And every one of those dickheads at Paddy's bought it, hook, line, and sinker.

As any exceptional actor will tell you, the most important element of acting is honesty. If you can fake that, you're golden. When you really think about it, what I've managed to pull off at Paddy's—playing the role of the world's best waitress for over a decade—is every bit as impressive as what Meryl Streep does when she makes a movie about a horny widow or a loudmouthed royal or something.

Not to take anything away from Meryl. I mean, she does decent work and half the time she gets an Oscar, but you want to hear her dirty secret? Once production wraps Meryl Streep gets to go home to her family and be just plain old Mel Streep, an unassuming housewife who enjoys playing pinochle and tending to her rosebushes and occasionally dressing up like Mar-

---

scumbags I deal with on a regular basis, she'd be the first to tell you that the slums of Calcutta ain't got a patch on the dumpy little shithole in South Philly where I sling drinks.

garet Thatcher for her husband's sexual gratification.[*] I, on the other hand, have not broken character for nearly half my friggin' life. Do I expect an Oscar for it? Frankly, I don't, because the academy has always been biased toward those working in the so-called professional acting world. But damn it, I don't care. That's my commitment to my craft, my unwavering dedication to the demanding role of Sweet Dee, the sexy, devil-may-care, world-class waitress with a heart of gold. Mel, on the other hand, turns the charm on and off like a cheap stripper. Or should I say, Streeper.[†]

Has this epic piece of performance art come at a cost? You bet your sweet ass it has. First, there's all the money I left on the table when I chose not to take the easy route and become an A-list Hollywood actress or Broadway star. Shit, I could have even made a nice living playing the hot wife married to some fat schlub in a vacuum cleaner commercial. But you know what? Any talentless boob with a pretty face and gorgeous figure can do that—just look at Julia Roberts! Me? I chose the road less traveled, and that has made, like, *tons* of difference. There's something poetic in that, don't you think?

Sadly, they don't give out Oscars for noncinematic achievements in thespianic excellence. If they did, I daresay I'd have a bunch of them on my mantel. I also daresay I could afford a mantel. And a house to put it in. And I could tell Dennis, Frank, Mac, and Charlie where to stick their stupid waitress job too.[‡]

Am I suggesting that a total lack of remuneration, respect, and recognition means that I halfway regret the ten years I've spent playing the role of Sweet Dee at Paddy's Pub? Not at all. I *completely* regret it. Seriously, every minute of it has been a living hell. If I don't get out soon and land a real acting gig I'll probably come in with an Uzi one day and you'll be reading about me on the news. But you know what that means? No matter what, I'm bound for fame. And you can take that to the bank, bitches.[§]

---

[*] I'm pretty sure I read something about that in the *National Enquirer.*

[†] Come at me, Mel. COME AT ME!

[‡] For the record, they can stick it in their butts. All the way in their butts.

[§] Do not take an Uzi to the bank.

Hi, guys, it's Dennis. Charlie really wanted to include some poetry based on his dream book in here. At first we told him no way. I mean, his dream book is pretty much one big cry for help if you ask me, and from the get-go we all agreed that showcasing anything like that in our international bestseller would make us look like we hang out with crazy people, which is not a good look. Eventually, however, we realized there was no way we were going to meet our contractually obligated word count on this book unless we started padding it out. So we tossed in anything we could find, no matter how much bullshit it was full of. And so, without further ado, please enjoy Charlie's ode to Hans Wermhatt, who apparently shoots at him from a biplane in his dreams. We also included a translation into English because we can.

HANS WERMHATT:

DREM BASTID

BYE CAT

UP N THE SKEY
A PLEN DOS FLEY
IZ RED WIZ SILVUR TRIM

ENSEYD THE PLEN
SIZZAMON HOOS NAYM
IZZ EVEL NVIL N GRIM

WIS WIKKET GLLEA
HE SCHOOTS AT ME
ENIAM FILLED WIT DRED

ZZZZZZ ZZZZZ

YT Y STILL SKREEM

N SUMTIME PEE THE BEDD

I RUN N RUN N RUN N RUN
N RUN N RUN N RUN

HE GUNNS N GUNNS N
GUNNZ N GUNNS N GUNNZ
N GUNNS N GUNNS

OM CHASED LEYK A RAT
BUT I'M NOT. IM CAT
I HATE YU SO MUC,
HANS WERMHATT

Hans Wermhatt:

Dream Bastard

A poem by Charlie Kelly

Up in the sky
A plane does fly
It's red with silver trim

Inside that plane
Sits a man whose name
Is evil and vile and grim

With wicked glee
He shoots at me
And I am filled with dread

It's all I dream
Yet I still scream
And sometimes pee the bed

I run and run and run and run
and run and run and run

He guns and guns and
guns and guns and guns
and guns and guns

I'm chased like a rat
But I'm not. I am cat
I hate you so much, Hans Wermhatt

17

Steal Your Way to a Better Life

By Frank

What's up, bitches? I got some financial advice you can't afford to pass up. People will tell you that the key to a good financial future is hard work and dedication, but that's a load of horseshit. There's only two surefire ways to make any real dough in this world, and that's whoring and stealing. Everyone's naturally inclined to do one or the other, even if they don't like to admit it.[*]

Now, I know what you're saying. You're saying, "That Frank Reynolds is a devilishly handsome fellow." And you make a good point. But guess what?

I'm onto you, whore!

---

[*] For the record, Charlie is a thief, Dennis is a whore, Mac is a thief, and Dee is a whore/thief (that's my girl!).

Any time I hear a compliment like that I automatically reach for my wallet. It's a conditioned response at this point, given the number of whores in my life. Or are you a thief? The craftiest thieves masquerade as whores to get your guard down. Then, right when you're passed out from plowing them for the last two and a half minutes, BAM, they strike.

My advice? It pays to be a thief. The hours are better and you don't have to get plowed all the time. The one drawback is that stealing is against the law, while I'm pretty sure whoring is legal now. I think they changed the law after that stupid Richard Gere movie with him and that pretty woman.[*]

But get this: While stealing is still technically against the law, the specific law that makes stealing illegal only applies to you if you get caught. I'll pause a second to let that sink in. <u>If you steal and you don't get caught, you don't have to go to jail.</u> Seriously. I've built an entire career on it, and I've only had to go to jail three or four times.

There are a few ways to avoid getting caught. The first is to not steal money. People tend to keep an eye on that stuff. My favorite thing to steal is companies. Best way to do that is find a company full of whores and tell them you can help them learn to be thieves and make some real money. Then, once you've got their trust, BAM! You steal the company. Stupid whores. Then all you gotta do is sell the thing and—bingo!—cash money, baby!!! And you know what that means: Daddy's taking a little whorecation.

Now, if you can't find a company to steal, there are plenty of other things. Drugs are a great thing to steal because the poor sap you stole them from can't go crying to the police. Plus, hey, drugs! Stealing people's identity is in vogue these days, but that was never really my style. I did steal Liam McPoyle's identity once, but it was all sweaty in there. I returned that shit in a hurry. Cars are pretty easy to steal. People just leave them lying around. To me that's pretty much asking for it. If

---

[*] *Nights in Rodanthe.* If it were still illegal, he would have been in jail for being a whore after making that pile of shit.

you can't find anything else, you can steal people's will to live, but the resale value on that's pretty low. I usually just do it for sport.

The other main way to avoid getting caught is to have partners. I always keep a partner or two around so I have someone to throw under the bus when the law comes knocking. You know that saying "Keep your friends close and your enemies closer"? A lot of people don't know the rest of it: "Keep your partners even closer than that, then at the last minute, snitch on them to the feds."

Now, reading this you might get the impression I'm some kind of unsavory person. I'm not!* I might steal, but I'm not mean about it. I don't pick on certain people. I'm what you call an equal opportunity thief. I've stolen from my best friends, I've stolen from my worst enemies, I've stolen from my whore wife, I've stolen from my brother, and I've stolen from my kids. I even stole from Roxy once, and she was the best whore I ever had. So don't judge me until you've walked a mile in my shoes. And when you get back and find out I've stolen *your* shoes, don't say I didn't warn you.

---

* Would I be giving you my best tricks if I was?

Refuse to Relent

By Mac

O ver the years the gang and I have dreamed up a number of what some cynical types might call "get-rich-quick schemes." But calling them that sells us short, and we are not short.[*] Sure they were all attempts to get rich, and to do so in a quick-like manner. But our efforts are not "schemes" perpetrated by shadowy sneaks who scurry around in the shadows. No, the business opportunities we create are done in the noble pursuit of an ideal, not some sort of striving and scraping attempt to make a quick buck. It's much like my pursuit of the perfect roundhouse kick. Yes, that's it precisely. Our moneymaking attempts are a series of business-oriented roundhouse kicks.

As anyone as skilled in combat as myself knows, it only takes one perfectly executed kick to shatter a man's jaw and render him a helpless quivering pile of patheticness who is forced to eat his meals through a straw while mumbling apologies like a heap of very guilty corned beef

---

[*] Except for Charlie. And Frank. But Dennis and I are not short, and we make up easily half the gang. More than half if you go by mass.

hash. But is the reason you practice roundhouse kicks so you can turn dudes to corned beef hash? Not at all. The Way of the Roundhouse is a calling unto itself. You do it for the discipline. You do it for the challenge. And you do it for the chicks.

It represents the kind of focus and high-minded idealitation that separates the winners from the losers. It's the difference between Hulk Hogan and all the dudes who lost to Hulk Hogan. It's the difference between Ric Flair and some whiny-ass bitch. You put a whiny-ass bitch in the octagon with Ric Flair and, believe me, Ric will pile-drive the shit out of that bitch. And get hella chicks.

All me and the gang have ever been trying to do is connect the Way of the Roundhouse to the Beach House of Business. It doesn't matter how many times our schemes don't end up taking us to that beach house. What matters is that we never give up and never lose faith in our incredible abilities. Some have called us relentless. I say no. We don't just relent a little less than others, we flat-out refuse to relent at all. And I'm here to tell you how you can too.

The key to perseverance is not listening when people tell you that you suck. And let me make this clear: They will tell you that you suck all the time. Even someone as consistently badass as me gets that crap. But, see, I know for a fact that I don't suck. I don't suck at martial arts, I don't suck at ocular pat-downs, I don't suck at building mass, and I definitely don't suck at Chardee MacDennis. But if you hear something like that often enough, there's a chance you might start to believe it. Luckily there's a simple solution: Don't listen. Ignore your friends and family when they criticize you. Believe me, it's made me a more happier, more confident person.

You also have to accept that all your roundhouse-kick business ideas are not gonna land. You will miss, and miss a lot. The gang certainly has. Sometimes badly. Usually it's when Charlie's involved. I sunk my life savings into Kitten Mittons, and it was a terrible, terrible mistake. But has he let consistent, abject failure stop him from pursuing his dream? No! He's pressed ahead, developing all the animal-themed products he can come up with, from Doggie Diapers to Cow Jeggings, the Skunk Tree, and, my favorite, the Rabbit Rabbit (a vibrator for rabbits). Are any of these inventions going to turn out to be Charlie's winning roundhouse kick? Probably not. Will they keep him occupied so that he doesn't try any of the *really* weird shit he's talked about, like launching a full-scale rodent-milking operation? That's what we're hoping.

And sometimes you have something that's a bona fide undeniable hit and it *still* doesn't take off. You just have to remember it's not your fault and you definitely don't suck. The Dick Towel should have been a sensation. Is it my fault we're stuck in a puritan hellscape? No way. And I still think we would have made a killing in the gasoline market if Charlie hadn't gotten carried away being a Wild Card.

But I haven't let these little setbacks keep me from moving forward. On the contrary, I'm always coming up with more great ideas. And I'm pretty sure this next idea is going to be the one that's so awesome it blows everyone's nips off. I'll tell you, but you have to promise to keep it a secret, cool? Okay, get this. What's the worst thing about sleeping? That's right, getting up to pee! That's why I've invented . . . wait for it . . .

The Bediaper

It's a mattress that absorbs urine, gently wicking it away from you throughout the night so you can continue to sleep peacefully. Pretty sweet in its own right, but check it out. Every six months or so, people are going to be lying in bed and say, "Whoa, this thing's getting a little damp." Because it'll be full of piss, see? It'll only work so long. So get this masterstroke: People will have to toss out the whole thing and buy a new one. It's a built-in market. And who's the only game in town? Oh, that'd be your old pal Mac. Soon as my bank loan comes through I'm going into production. Let me know how many I can put you down for. Remember to buy a spare!

Charlie Work

and How to

Avoid It

By Dennis

I believe it was the great German psychologist Karl Malden who opined that "work is the curse of the drinking class." I got a million great quotes like that up in the old noggin, little nuggets of gold I like to bestow on the people when they need a little wisdom to get them through the day. Still, from time to time certain people have questioned the accuracy of my sourcing. And to them I say, "Sourcing? Oh, you mean the miracle of evolution sitting in my skull?" I don't need to look something up to know it's true.

Now, if I were slavishly devoted to accuracy and punctiliousness, I suppose I could have looked up the aforementioned quote to confirm its accuracy, but, frankly, it seemed like too much work. Especially after I already exerted myself deciding whether to look up "punctiliousness." (Pretty sure it means "the state of having just the right amount of punctuation.") But seriously, am I really supposed to sit around verifying things I know are true when I could be pounding cold brews and hot tail instead? Let's face facts: There are two kinds of people in this world: those who sweat the small stuff, and those who have the balls not to.

The point I'm trying to make here is that work is for suckers, or, as we call them down at Paddy's Pub, Charlie. To his credit, that poor, ignorant, trash-eating bastard doesn't know any better. To him, work isn't the odious impediment to nonstop carnal pleasure and wild drunkenness that I've always known it to be, but rather something that a rodent-obsessed urchin with scant career prospects willingly endures out of a misguided sense of duty to serve the common good. And sure, that's sad in a way. But it's the kind of delusional thinking that keeps my bar's toilets clean. So when you think about it, it's actually pretty happy.

Even in this modern age, with a seemingly endless stream of easily exploitable labor crossing the Mexican border into our country every day, it's amazing how few degenerates are willing to degrade themselves doing Charlie Work. I'm talking about the menial and disgusting and totally beneath-me tasks necessary to keep a place like Paddy's Pub running smoothly: Cleaning toilets. Killing rats. Burning trash. Mopping up blood. Removing corpses. Changing the kegs.

Look, I'd sooner cut off my own genitals before I'd ever do something like spackle up the glory hole in the men's room stall at Paddy's. I mean, I had my dick in that hole, for chrissakes. But that's just it, isn't it? In life there are hole bangers and hole fixers. I'm a banger, not a fixer, and, like Jack Frost said, "that has made all the diffidence."

The Way
of the
Wild Card

By Charlie (as told to Artemis)

Every great crew in history has divided its members into the same basic roles: the Brains, the Looks, the Muscle, the Useless Chick, and finally, most importantly, the Wild Card. I, Charlie, am the Wild Card in our crew, and I gotta tell you it's pretty awesome. The most awesome thing about being the Wild Card of the Paddy's Pub crew is that unlike the Brains (Mac), the Looks (Dennis), the Muscle (Frank), and the Useless Chick (duh), I don't have to do anything. It's not that I *don't* do anything. Shit, I do stuff all the time. It's that I don't *have to*. That's why I wrote "have to" in the first place. Well, actually, I only said it, Artemis wrote it. Thanks,

Artemis.[*] You know, Artemis, I feel like I'm getting the hang of this writing thing now.[†] But just think if I hadn't said "have to" there. You'd be totally confused right now and be all, like, how can five people have a great crew when one-fifth of it isn't doing anything?[‡] And while you were sitting there all jammed up about me saying I don't do anything, I *would* do something, and that something would be awesome and probably dangerous and you'd never see it coming until it was too late.

Maybe I'd start calling you Angelo. That's not your name. And it doesn't suit you.[§] But I'd do it. And that's doing something. Cuz I'm the Wild Card. There doesn't have to be a reason behind anything I do. If there's one thing you can count on, it's me not counting. On. One. Thing. To. Count. On. Ever. Again. Again. Again. Again.[**]

Wow, that was pretty deep. I just realized rat traps that I don't even need the words I string together cheese into sentences to go together Uncle Jack fur toilet.

Like a snake or a jackalope, the Wild Card is completely unpredictable. He's the kind of guy who'll tap his brakes like he's gonna stop at the stop sign but then WILD CARD! He just blows right through it and clips a pedestrian, and then when the cop asks him if he's been drinking, instead of lying and saying no like you'd expect a normal person to do, he turns around and says yeah, he's wasted and high on airplane glue.

---

[*] ARTEMIS: You're welcome, Charlie.

[†] ARTEMIS: You're definitely coming along, Charlie.

[‡] ARTEMIS: That's two-fifths if you count Dee.

[§] ARTEMIS: Like, at *all*.

[**] ARTEMIS: Charlie said "again" here, about thirty or forty times, alternating from giggling wildly to being extremely serious. He's not messing around about this Wild Card stuff. Anyway, I can't be bothered to write all of them down and anyway, I wouldn't be able to convey the proper inflection, so you'd lose a lot of the meaning. There are some things you just need to be present for. I mean really *present*.

Which—WILD CARD!—is also a lie. He only had five beers and it was computer duster spray, not airplane glue. Stupid cops.

In conclusion I'd like to leave you with a few powerful and inspirational words of wisdom that will help motivate you for the rest of your life. But I'm not going to. In fact, I'm not going to leave you period, Angelo. I'm just gonna keep writing and writing and writing and writing and writing until your eyes bleed and you can't handle me writing any more anymore. And the reason I'll do that is that there *is* no reason to do it. Nor is there a reason not to not do it. Or to not not not not do it. Just like there's no reason for me to put this ® here or to smegle house frugen zee poopadoodle. I beat to my own fife. And that, my dear bitches, is the Way of the Wild Card.

QUIZ
QUORNER

By Frank

Hey, it's Frank. The guys asked me to write up the finance quiz for the end of this section, because seriously, you think one of those jamokes is gonna do it? Mac and Dennis don't know an asset from an asshole. You'd think that having owned a bar for so many years they would've acquired some basic understanding of economics if only by accident. But not these knuckleheads. They're as terrible at managing money as they are at every other important thing in life. Except for getting trashed. They're a regular bunch of geniuses when it comes to that.

Take that time Paddy's got audited. I'm cooking the books trying to keep us all outta jail and I ask Mac a simple question about the bar's liquidity ratio. Guy looks at me like I'm speaking friggin' Chinese. Then he sits there for six hours, not saying a word, going beer for beer with me while I fudge the numbers. He got so drunk, he didn't even notice when I pissed all over myself and the file folder with the phony receipts we needed for the IRS. Like I said, not so good with numbers, but he's great at getting drunk. I still have no idea how *he* didn't piss himself that day. But we all have our talents.

Speaking of the Chinese, pretty soon those slick sonofabitches are gonna be running the whole goddamn shithouse. Mark my words, we're all screwed. Those Chinese, they're not like the lazy bastards we got over here. They work harder and for a lot less money, especially the ones being forced to by the Chinese government. Which is to say pretty much all of them. Hell, I just read in the paper that the Chinese are already holding something like $4 gazillion in foreign exchange reserves. Do you have any idea what that means? You probably don't, do you? Too busy dicking around watching videos of cats playing drums on the Facetube. See, what'd I tell you? We're screwed.

Anyway, here's the quiz the dipshits told me to do. It's not gonna help you get rich, so don't get your hopes up. All I did was spend five minutes making up some bullshit questions and answers. Check off whatever the hell answers you want. It's not going to matter when the Chinese come for us. The end is near, America. This country's going down the tube. You want to do something useful with your brain? Learn to say "You want fries with that?" in Mandarin.

ASSESSING YOUR FINANCIAL

LITERACY

1. When the Chinese eventually call in America's debts and try to take over the country, the best thing we can do is . . .

   ❏   a. bomb the shit outta Beijing.

   ❏   b. bomb the shit outta Shanghai.

   ❏   c. bomb the shit outta Hong Kong.

   ❏   d. bang the shit outta all the hot Chinese women that'll be moving in.

2. A typical nickname for a ruthless financial wizard is . . .

   ❏   a. Dr. Mantis Toboggan.

   ❏   b. Frankie Fast Hands.

   ❏   c. The Muscle.

   ❏   d. The Warthog.

   ❏   e. The Philly Frenetic.

3. Women and minorities in the workplace . . .

   ❏   a. are a valuable addition to the workforce.

   ❏   b. are essential when you need coffee or a cocktail.

   ❏   c. need to stop taking jobs from poor, defenseless white men.

   ❑   d. need to tone down their protests. We get
               it, you're pissed about the way you've
               been treated. Now get me that beer I
               asked for.

4. Examples of sound investment opportunities include (check all that apply):

  ❑   a. A boat (any condition).
  ❑   b. Dick Towels.
  ❑   c. Kitten Mittons.
  ❑   d. Fight Milk.
  ❑   e. Child beauty pageants.
  ❑   f. Door-to-door wet-vac sales.
  ❑   g. Delaware River sewage runoff crabs.
  ❑   h. Paddy's Dollars.
  ❑   i. *Lethal Weapon 5.*
  ❑   j. Sweatshops in Vietnam.
  ❑   k. Nightclubs opened with your brother, Gino.
  ❑   l. A ~~rape~~ surveillance van.
  ❑   m. Virus videos.
  ❑   n. Dennis and Dee's podcast.
  ❑   o. Official Paddy's Pub–branded thongs.
  ❑   p. Public access news shows.
  ❑   q. Magnum condoms (if you're investing in them to impress a pharmacist).
  ❑   r. Band equipment and hotel expenses for Chemical Toilet.
  ❑   s. *Lethal Weapon 6.*

❏ t. Official Paddy's Pub–branded hard-boiled eggs.

❏ u. Unofficial Paddy's Pub–branded hard-boiled eggs.

❏ v. An erotic memoir based on Dennis's life.

❏ w. The Gun Shot.

❏ x. The Shot Gun.

❏ y. Sweatshops in Philly.

❏ z. A billboard for the bar.

❏ 1. Repossessed homes (with or without people living in them).

❏ 2. Dennis's male escort business.

❏ 3. *Lethal Weapon 7.*

❏ 4. U.S. Treasury bonds.

❏ 5. Nudie pens.

❏ 6. Whores.

5. The best way to turn a company around is to . . .

❏ a. blow through the place like a friggin' tornado and cut the crust off the shit sandwich (a.k.a. fire all the assholes).

❏ b. woo wealthy Asian investors by taking them to a fancy dinner where they serve sushi on a naked broad.

❏ c. employ the three L's: lie, lie, lie.

❏ d. empty all of its bank accounts and declare Chapter 11. Suckers.[*]

---

[*] I never said it had to be a positive turnaround.

6. What is the typical relationship between interest rates and bond prices?

- ❏ a. This is not the "Relationships" section.
- ❏ b. Blow me.
- ❏ c. All of the above.

7. Which of the following is the best definition of "junk bond"?

- ❏ a. Timothy Dalton.
- ❏ b. A bond that is rated "below investment grade" by rating agencies.
- ❏ c. The kinship shared by all heroin addicts.
- ❏ d. The epoxy you use to glue missing pieces of your dong back on after a rough night.

8. True or false: My monthly earnings exceed my monthly expenses by 30 percent or more.

- ❏ a. True, I am a financial wizard who, though small in stature, is worshipped like a colossus and can get any whore he wants.
- ❏ b. True, but only because I work in a place where I drink for free.
- ❏ c. False. I am a dead-end alcoholic sociopath running a bar in South Philly.

9. Is the average after-tax yield of your savings and investments greater than the rate of inflation?

- ❏ a. Are you talking about the inflation of my prostate?
- ❏ b. Because my diet is heavy on packaged meat products.

❏ c. Look, I spend my money on whores. Is that what you're getting at?

❏ d. Pass.

10. Credit card debt is . . .

❏ a. another way for big business to screw the little guy.

❏ b. the proud underwriter of the American dream: a TV big enough to watch porn on at 1:1 scale.

❏ c. sometimes the only way to keep a good whore working.

11. Personal retirement accounts are . . .

❏ a. a good way to defer taxes on earned income.

❏ b. a good way to think about dying all the time. No thanks.

❏ c. future whore money.

❏ d. a myth.

12. My will is . . .

❏ a. an important part of planning for the well-being of those I leave behind.

❏ b. the only thing keeping Dennis and Dee from offing me.

❏ c. a good way to mess with people after I die.

❏ d. law.

13. What are the benefits of saving a little money from every paycheck?

❏ a. There are numerous benefits, so long as the paycheck you're taking that money from isn't yours.

❏ b. There are none. You know the old saying "You can't take it with you"? I agree with that 100 percent. In fact, I have a corollary: "I ain't leaving any of it behind either. And sure as shit not to those ungrateful sonofabitch kids of mine."

❏ c. Not becoming friggin' Cricket.

❏ d. Save up enough money from a legit job, and maybe during the lean times you won't have to resort to doing anything desperate to survive . . . like writing a goddamn self-help book.

PART III

Fashion and Personal Grooming

Makeup:
A Man's Game

By Dennis

This modern era we live in has brought with it a lot of changes to everyday life. Who today could imagine a world without cell phones, e-mail, or hidden video cameras? But the most important change our generation has lived through exists on a whole other level of importance. That's right, I'm talking about makeup for men.

There once was a dark time when only women wore the stuff, which, if you ask me, is completely unfair. If you look at history, everything's always gone women's way. Well it's time for a little thing called gender equality, ladies. Try to keep up. Men wear makeup now, and you're just going to have to deal with it.

Now, I say men, but it's not all men. Yet. Today, it's really just your more evolved sex beasts who take advantage of it. You know, the men who aren't afraid to show the world that we're here and we're super bangable. The face is the billboard that sells the body, gentlemen. If that thing doesn't pop off the rack, then you ain't selling shit.

And I know what you're thinking. You're thinking, "Dennis, you have the face of an angel! Who would presume to put makeup on an angel?" An aesthetic genius, that's who. I'd like to introduce you to a little concept I like to call Perfection Plus. That's what happens when you take something that's already exceptional and find a way to knock it even higher into the stratosphere. Sure, you might make a few people's heads explode from the sheer visual overload, but that's just the price the world has to pay for greatness.

Now, before we go further, please know that I'm fully aware that Perfection Plus won't apply to most of you reading this. No problem. Most ordinaries have weak points. You can use these techniques to shore up those glaring flaws. That said, I know there's at least one guy out there for whom Perfection Plus is the perfect solution. I'm talking to you, Dennis Reynolds, you sleek, catlike walking distillate of desire. Wait, did I just do a shout-out to myself in a book I was writing precisely so I could masturbate to it later?

I don't know . . . did I?

Now where was I? Oh yeah. Makeup.

It's pretty simple stuff, really; we can break it down into three basic categories:

1.   Face makeup

The important thing here is subtlety. You want to bring out the natural beauty of your features, but not so much that people get suspicious. There is a natural prejudice in the world against those of us who are called to the heights of beauty. Believe me, I've got stories. You run afoul of that at your peril. Basically, less evolved dudes tend to get weirded out if they can tell you're wearing mascara. Go easy.

2. Ab makeup

If you head out for a day at the beach without proper ab makeup, you only have yourself to blame when you don't end up bringing home the bacon. And by "bacon" I mean puss. Fortunately, applying ab makeup is pretty simple. Start off by applying a base across your entire torso, then fill in some definition. I have a natural six-pack, so it's really more about bringing out the highlights, but don't be afraid to paint one in freehand on your disgusting, flabby gut. Just use a slightly darker shade than your base and trace in a central line up and down. Now fill in some broad, curved lines out toward the sides and . . . oh, who am I kidding? You look like fat Skeletor now. Just keep your shirt on, okay?

3. Love makeup

There's no way to sugarcoat this. I'm talking about makeup for your penis. This is all about enhancing the lesser qualities of your particular shaft. There is a real art to this one, but the crux of it is often in the shadowing and definition. Much like the abs, giving your penis the proper enhancements can be both effective and fun! If you have a small head, shadow the shaft to make it seem smaller and the head appear larger. If you have messy veins, color them in to create a unified flesh tone. If your lover likes veins, draw more. You get the gist. Of course if your skin is of the darker persuasion, you're going to want to lighten things up down there. Just make sure you go with a beige or other off-white. You don't want to blind anyone.

Hey, remember when I said there was no way to sugarcoat this? That's not strictly true. Advanced practitioners of the art of donghancement have been known to mix a little sugar and vanilla into their foundation to encourage ladies to satisfy their sweet tooth while satisfying them. That's just a little protip from one sex beast to another. Use it in good health. Unless this is more of an in-the-woods outdoors sort of bang you have planned, in which case keep it unflavored. No one likes ants at a picnic. Especially when that picnic is your junk. And for the love of god, laser your pubes off, you animal.

America:
Love It or Sleeve It

A Treatise on the Right to Bare Arms

By Mac

As you can probably guess, I've never been a fan of rules. That's because rules are, by their very nature, designed to restrict our personal liberties. They're like sleeves on Chuck Norris's shirt. Sleeves limit Chuck's range of motion, and that's a dangerous game, friend. I'm not down with rules the same way I'm not down with shirtsleeves. By not wearing them (rules and sleeves), I'm letting the rest of the world know just how much I love America.

What's the first thing you notice when you turn on the news and see all those angry motherfuckers in Iran and Iraq and France? All wearing sleeves. Every last one. Why? Because they've been oppressed so long they don't know what freedom feels like anymore. They're like savages, only with extra clothes on instead of not enough.

America has been all about Freedom from the very beginning Pilgrim times. Do you think the founding fathers gave a shit about rules? No way! They were too busy writing our Constitution to waste time making up a bunch of rules.

And don't get me started on Pilgrims. Those dudes partied so hard they ended up with buckles on their hats. I've woken up with my shoes on and my pants off a few times, but never with a goddamn buckle on my hat. That is some next-level shit.

Anyway, it was George King who always had all the rules, but when he tried to jam us up with them, Jefferson and Lincoln and their boys were like, "Bro! Why don't you take your funny accent and your fancy boy wigs and your stupid rules and go back to *der Motherland* where you came from. We're just gonna stay here and get high on peyote with our new Indian friends."

But this King dude turned out to be a total jabroni and was all like, "Cheerio, you are my subjects. Remain loyal to the crown or die." And we were all, "Bring it, bitch!" and King's like, "Tallyho!" But he didn't count on us being such badasses, what with all the time in the desert eating peyote and the mental toughness that brings, not to mention the spirit animals. The founding fathers had mad spirit animals. Jefferson could turn into a mongoose and Washington could turn into an eagle (duh). And you never saw fear like in an army that sees an eagle carrying a mongoose and is headed straight at 'em. Anyway, long story short, we kicked some serious English ass and from that moment on, every man, woman, and child in this country has lived free or died and sometimes both.

But the most important thing about America is that we learn from the past. So what did we learn from the Revolutionary War? A lot. We learned that the British are pretty much the pansies they sound like they'd be. We learned that Indians are great warriors with awesome drugs and that they have tons of land that's just sitting around waiting for their new friends to live on it. And that America is the greatest and freest and noblest country the world has ever known. And that means we don't have to care about what anyone else has to say, and that's why we don't have to follow rules, and we certainly don't need to wear sleeves.

23

The Nightman

By Frank and Charlie

Yo, Frank here. A couple of years ago Charlie wrote one of those rock operas that were big in the seventies—you know, like *Jesus Christ Superstar*. Only, Charlie didn't write *The Nightman Cometh* because he wanted it to become a Broadway hit. Hell, I'm pretty sure he didn't give a shit if anyone liked it at all really. Except for one person, that is. Charlie wrote that musical to impress the waitress and get her to marry him. It didn't work out too good.

The weird thing is, Charlie didn't end up putting the song that inspired the musical into the actual show. I think that's why the show bombed, actually. The only time "The Nightman" was ever performed was at a talent show we had a few years back. Went over like a charm that night, let me tell you. We even had the music critic from the *Philadelphia Inquirer* down here when we performed it, thanks to some brilliant PR shenanigans on my part.[*] The *Inquirer* guy called it "a surprisingly

---

[*] I sent a messenger-delivered note telling him that Holland Oates was playing a secret show at Paddy's that night.

accomplished debut that nevertheless made me throw up in my mouth."
I was confused about how he closed out the piece, though: "Someone
should really call the police." What the hell is he so hot about? This is a
song of friendship, about two men sharing the night. The police always
screw stuff like that up when they get involved. Maybe he was talking
about Paddy's fire safety regulations or the pickled eggs we keep behind
the bar. Actually I bet it was the pickled eggs. Those things are more
dangerous than my .38.

Anyway, I think if Charlie had kept "The Nightman" in, *The
Nightman Cometh* could have made it to Broadway. Instead, it just
broke his heart. And Charlie was insistent that we include the lyrics
in the book. He says it's uplifting. The kind of song that's "tailor-made
for someone in desperate need of help." And since Charlie's the one
who got us this book deal in the first place, what the hell, we'll put it
in. We couldn't figure out what section it should go in, so we put it in
"Fashion and Personal Grooming."* So here's Charlie's original song,
as translated by Artemis.

---

* According to Dennis, nine-tenths of being a successful rock and roller is looking good.

"The Nightman"
Music and lyrics by Charlie Kelly

Nightman, sneaky and mean
Spider inside my dreams, I think I love you
You make me wanna cry
You make me wanna die
I love you I love you
I love you I love you
I love you, Nightman

Every night you come into my room
And pin me down
With your strong arms
You pin me down
And I try to fight you
You come inside me
You fill me up and I become the Nightman

It's just two men sharing the night
It might seem wrong
But it's just right!
It's just two men sharing each other
It's just two men like loving brothers
One on top and one on bottom
One is inside and one is out
One is screaming he's so happy
The other's screaming a passionate shout

It's the Nightman
The feelings so wrong and right, man
They're feeling so wrong and right, man

I can't fight you, man
When you come inside me
And pin me down with your strong hands
And I become the Night
The passionate passionate Nightman

And that's it. Nothing to see here, folks. People want to get weird about stuff and they find stupid made-up reasons. Now, sorry to cut this short, but I gotta head back to the apartment. Charlie and I are having a Night Crawlers marathon, and you can't be late to that or you get docked thirty points and have to start the next five matches with the other guy on your back. And if you ask me, that's no way to play Night Crawlers.

24

Blackface

Versus

Whiteface

By Mac, Dennis, and Frank

Dennis: —why you even brought up this whiteface versus black-face shit again. It's stupid. We have much more pressing matters to . . . wait, why are you recording this?

Mac: Because, Dennis, it's not stupid. In fact, it's the polar opposite of stupid—it's important.

Frank: Wouldn't smart be the polar opposite of stupid?

Dennis: Frank's right. Important is not the polar opposite of stupid. Smart, yes. Intelligent, sure. Brilliant, absolutely. But important? Not even close. Ironically, Mac, it turns out your statement on stupidity was an incredibly stupid thing to say.

Mac: No way. They're definitely opposites, bro.

Dennis: No, they are definitely not, bro. And even if they were, you said they're *polar* opposites, which is a superlative. That, my friend, is a whole 'nother level of opposite.

Frank: You can't get no more opposite than that . . .

Dennis: Back me up, Frank. I think it's safe to say that not only is our linguistically challenged friend here woefully uninformed about the dynamics of oppositism, he also has no idea what "polar" means either.

Frank: No friggin' clue.

Mac: Bullshit! Of course I know what "polar" means! Now let's get back to—

Dennis: What does it mean?

Mac: What?

Dennis: What does "polar" mean?

Frank: Yeah, let's hear it, Mister Important.

Mac: Goddamn it, I don't want to talk about the meaning of "polar"! This conversation is supposed to be about whiteface versus blackface.

Dennis: Ah, but it took an unexpected turn, didn't it? Ended up being a discussion about the intricacies of language and how some people have a hard time with them. Would you say that's the *polar opposite* of what we were supposed to be talking about, Mac?

[extended silence]

Frank: He don't know what "polar" means.

Dennis: Definitely not . . .

Mac: "Straight," goddamn it!

Dennis: What's that now?

Mac: "Straight"! "Polar" means "straight"!

Frank: Huh?

Mac: Like how a pole is a straight . . . line. You go straight to somewhere from somewhere else, like on the Polar Express.

Frank: And I'm the dumbass?

Dennis: Dude, seriously?

Mac: I don't know why you guys feel the need to always attack, attack, attack! Look, we have a book to write—and we are waaaaay behind schedule, I might add. Is it too much to ask you guys to stop attacking me about this stupid language shit so that we can have an intelligent conversation about whether blackface or whiteface is more offensive? Is that too much to goddamn ask?!!!

Dennis: Maybe you need to calm down a little.

Mac: What?!!! Bro, I'm totally calm!!!

Dennis: No, you're not.

Frank: You're the polar opposite of calm.

Dennis: Oh, zing! Good one, Frank!

[*loud banging noise, possibly a chair falling over*]

Dennis: Wait, Mac, where you going? We're just messing with ya . . .

[*sound of door slamming*]

Frank: He just went polar—*straight*—out the door! Get it?

Dennis: Yeah, I get it.

Frank: Mac makes it so easy.

Dennis: So what were we talking about again?

Frank: I dunno. Something stupid, probably.

Dennis: Was it about having some beers? 'Cause that's what I want it to be about.

Frank: Sounds about right.

Dennis: Always does.

[*sound of liquid being poured and clinking glasses*]

EDITOR'S NOTE: I originally thought this audio recording had been submitted in error as it begins halfway through a sentence and contains several highly offensive lines of reasoning. When I ran the transcript by Mr. Kelly, however, he briefly scanned it and pronounced it "perfect." When I pointed out he might need to run it by his fellow coauthors he became agitated and began accusing me of being a "naysayer," then stuck his fingers in his ears, loudly saying, "La la la la, can't hear you, naysayer, say all the nays you want." The transcript is presented here unexpurgated, in its entirety. I have placed it in the fashion section because it is ostensibly about appearance (though in actuality it appears to be about ignorance, pettiness, and bullying).

How to Look
Like a Giant Bird

By Dee

Okay, Damon, I don't know who you think you are, but just because you're the editor of this dumb-ass book, apparently you think that makes it okay to lord it over the creatives down here in the trenches. Remember us? The ones who do the real work? Yeah, I get it. You probably went to Harvard and got some goddamn literature degree and wear a monocle and you think that gives you license to just piss all over everyone and everything you don't like. But you know what, Damon? I don't give a damn about your fancy degree. In fact I'm beginning to think you might be a Grade-A jerk.

I mean, I already came up with some pretty amazing pieces for the earlier sections. But do you call to tell me how brilliant I am? No. Do you e-mail me, thanking me for my hard work? Absolutely not. Not your style, is it, Damon? No, you turn around and PRESUME to assign me *this* nonsense I'm writing right now. I mean, what the hell kind of topic is "how to look like a giant bird" anyway? It doesn't even make sense. It has nothing to do with anything, let alone fashion and personal grooming. I'm guessing that it's got some kind of obscure metaphoric analogous meaning to you. Something you picked up in your Chaucer class perhaps? Oh look at me, I'm a fancy literary editor in fancy New York City with my fancy monocle assigning fancy stories. Well you know what? I don't think it's so fancy. You heard me. I think it's god-damn lame. Which means it should have been assigned to Charlie.

And I'd tell you myself if I knew how to get in touch with you directly, but looks like you're such a biiiig swinging-dick New York City book editor type that you don't use e-mail or make phone calls like us serfs. Oh no, Damon, all of your precious communications are handled via *messenger* service. Fancy! Is that how they did things at boarding school? You can't hide forever, though. One of these times I'm going to be here when one of your packets arrives and I'm going to get your return address and I'm going to take a bus to New York City and come tell you to your big, fat, stupid, rich, attractive face what you can do with your bullshit giant-bird assignment. You can write it yourself, Damon. You know why? Because you're a turkey, Damon. And I can't think of anyone better than a turkey to write about how to look like a giant bird.

Feeling the burn a little there, Damon? Oh, I'm sorry about that. I had no idea.

Except I'm not sorry! And I had every idea! That's a little thing I like to call *sarcasm*. Learned it in a little thing I like to call *college* (which I very nearly finished) and it's just one of the many tools I have at my literary disposal. And make no mistake, I will use them all in the service of destroying you.

See, I've got more important things to offer the world. Stuff that can actually help people. I'm a strong, photogenic female role model who valiantly overcame a debilitating childhood affliction to become an accomplished actress, teacher, and artist. The people who buy this book will be trying to better themselves, and who *better* (see what I did there?) to help them with that than me? I'm a heart-attack survivor and a single mother who made the courageous decision to give up my child and only occasionally claim him as a dependent on my tax returns.

You wanna look like a giant bird? You think that'll help you get ahead in the book business? Okay, fine. Get some yellow cardboard and make a beak out of it. Then tar and feather yourself. Congratulations, jerk, you're the new editor in chief of Random Penguin Collins House Press! Have fun with all the random penguins, Damon! Bet those guys are super fun to hang out with while they're regurgitating meals into their babies' mouths. Hey, whatever it takes to get you off. You want to regurgitate your lunch on a random penguin, be my guest.

Unless you are cute. And rich. In which case this essay is just the first step in our hot-and-cold will-she-won't-she courtship that wouldn't be out of place in a Nora Ephron movie. Oh, we'll look back on this one day and laugh, won't we, Damon? The grandkids will roll their eyes in mock annoyance because they love hearing it for the gajillionth time at Christmas.

But not yet. Right now my hate burns for you with the white-hot fury of a million suns. I hope you die in a fire.

When Charlie Met

Holland Oates

EDITOR'S NOTE: I am fully aware that this has nothing to do with fashion or personal grooming. Apparently, the authors have no coherent thoughts or advice for this section beyond man makeup. I placed this chapter here because, well, fuck it. If editing this book has taught me anything it's that people are uncaring sociopaths, life is cruel and cold, and we all die alone.

Whattup, suckers, Dee all up in ya grill pans. Just got a piece of bad news. Turns out my shit-luck streak remains unbroken. Apparently, Rock and Roll Hall of Famer John Oates got lost on his way to a gig yesterday and ended up coming into Paddy's for directions . . . WHEN I WASN'T THERE. Goddamn stupid shitballs!!! He could have been my ticket out of this hellhole! For Christ's sake, I was born to bone rock stars! I'd have rocked his world! Plus he's from Philly, so we probably have tons in common besides both being artists and both being great at boning. Like a hatred of Philly.

Mrs. Deandra Reynolds Oates. Goddamn if that doesn't just sound right.

Anyway, Charlie was the only one in the bar when John came in. He recognized him right away, flipped out, and recorded the whole encounter and said I should submit it to the transcriber people in New York, with some kind of intro. I can't even bring myself to listen to it before I send it off, so here's my intro:

> **Charlie is a no-good dickbag who knows his friend Dee has a crush on John Oates and should have called her immediately the moment John Oates stepped into the bar. Instead he talked to him. And probably made him puke with his goddamned cheese breath. Asshole.**

Charlie: Man, this is incredible!

John Oates: Hey, uh, why are you holding that phone in front of my face?

Charlie: I'm recording our interview!

Oates: This isn't an interview. I just need directions to the Tower Theater.

Charlie: Of all the gin joints in all the Philadelphias in all the worlds, Holland Oates walks into mine.

Oates: Listen, I'm kind of in a hurry here . . .

Charlie: It's just weird, you know? Dennis and I were listening to the radio the other day and "Rich Girl" came on and he was like, "Aw, this shit sucks balls, let's put on Simon O'Garfunkel," but I was like, "Goddamn it, dude, you're crazy, there's only one man who can rock this hard and that's Holland Oates."

Oates: Um, well I appreciate it, but . . . you do know we're a duo, right?

Charlie: Well sure! I mean, you probably have a whole band, am I right? Important guy like Holland Oates has to have a drummer and a fiddler and all kinds of other guys around. But without a front man, without Holland Oates, well, the rest of those guys don't mean shit.

Oates: My name's John. John Oates. I'm half of *Hall* & Oates.

Charlie: Oh man, I get you. That's so cool. You get low. Hey, I do too. Sometimes you don't feel like Holland Oates, you just feel like a regular Oates. Like the most regular kind of Oates there is, you know, *John* Oates. Shit, that's deep. But seriously, I've been there. Today, I'd say I'm only about a third of Charlie Kelly. Actually, you know what? Today, I'm *John* Kelly. I feel you, bro. Hey, how 'bout a beer?

Oates: I can't. My gig. I gotta take off—

Charlie: Naw, come on, I insist! One bottle of Budweiser on the house for Mr. Holland Oates! Got it right here.

Oates: That's . . . already opened.

Charlie: Yeah, I got really drunk last night and I couldn't finish. Moderation! Important, right? But the other half of this is perfectly good beer.

Oates: Um, I'm gonna pass.

Charlie: You're in the Rock and Roll Hall of Fame and you're going to pass on a free beer?

Oates: Half beer.

Charlie: Half beer, whatever. Geez! God! Was it something I said? I mean, you come in here and I'm a little starstruck is all. It's not like I'm some crazy person who's gonna hit you over the head with this rat stick and chain you up to one of the mannequins I keep in the basement over by the boiler and make you sing me songs forever and ever and ever and ever while I care for you like my own little life-size doll.

Oates: Hey, man, you keep waving that bat around. It's really making me kind of uncomfortable.

Charlie: Bat?

Oates: Yeah, the bat in your hand. With the nails sticking out of it?

Charlie: Oh! No. This isn't a bat. It's a rat stick. And those are death spikes, not nails. Understandable mistake, though. You being a famous musician and all. Would I be right in assuming you probably don't kill your own rats anymore?

Oates: I'm not . . . sure . . . I . . .

Charlie: Wait a second, Holland. Are you telling me you *don't* already have someone on staff to kill your rats? Cuz seriously, dude, I will walk out of here right now with you and work for you and you'll never have to worry about rats or mold, or cleaning out glory holes or anything like that ever again.

Oates: It's okay, I already have a . . . rat killer.

Charlie: Oh yeah? What's his name?

Oates: His name?

Charlie: Uh, yeah! Rat killers have names, dude. And it's a pretty small world. I probably know him. Come on, I gotta know who snaked my dream gig.

Oates: Look, I don't know if we should be talking about this . . .

Charlie: Oh my god, you're right. I'm sorry. This is totally inappropriate. Rat killer–client privilege. I get it. Sorry. I'm acting like an idiot. I'm just nervous.

Oates: It's okay. Just try and stay calm. You're not an idiot.

Charlie: I'm not!

Oates: That's what I said.

Charlie: I know!

Oates: Good.

Charlie: Seriously, though, I'm, like, your *biggest* fan.

Oates: Oh man, that's great. That's so great.

Charlie: What's your favorite song of yours?

Oates: Oh, well, it's so hard to pick a favorite . . .

Charlie: Tell me!

Oates: Okay, okay, okay . . . just lower the bat.

Charlie: Rat stick.

Oates: Right. Lower the . . . rat stick. Thank you. I think "Maneater" is one of our best.

Charlie: Hmm. I don't think I know that one. How 'bout one of the, like, popular ones.

Oates: Sure, okay. "You Make My Dreams Come True."

Charlie: Are you serious?

Oates: Yes.

Charlie: I feel the same way about you!

Oates: You wha . . . Oh no, no, no . . . That's the name of a song of ours . . . of mine.

Charlie: Can you sing it for me?

Oates: I have to, uh, save my voice. You know, for tonight's show.

Charlie: Oh, riiiight. I'd love to come to that.

Oates: You would?

Charlie: Yeah! You know what? If you wanted, I could come out early and clear the place of rats for you. Wait, does your rat guy travel with you?

Oates: He does.

Charlie: But I tell ya, there's nothing like having two guys on a job, just two men in the dark swinging their sticks, covered in rat guts, lost in their work.

Oates: You know, I would totally invite you to the show, but my rat guy is pretty insecure. He sees a real pro like you in the building, he'll think I'm trying to show him the door. You understand, right?

Charlie: Oh, sure, totally. I get that. It's cool. Can I ask you for one other thing then? Would you mind dedicating my favorite song of yours to me tonight?

Oates: Sure. Anything you want, so long as you'll let me leave. What song?

Charlie: "Against All Odds."

Oates: But that's . . .

Charlie: What?

Oates: . . . a great . . . song!

Charlie: It really is, isn't it!

Oates: Yup! Absolutely. All right, I'm gonna go now. See ya.

Charlie: Oh, hey, Holland? One more thing . . .

Oates: Seriously?

Charlie: I think you should shave your mustache back on.

Oates: Sure thing, buddy. Sure thing.

QUIZ
QUORNER

By Dennis

N oted fashion icon and reverse sexist Coco Chanel famously said, "A girl should be two things: classy and fabulous." Hey, Coco! What about the legions of heartbroken little boys out there who heard that and thought, "What about me, Coco Chanel? WHAT ABOUT ME?!! I can't be classy and fabulous too, just because I have this sad piece of flesh hanging between my legs?"

Well, boys, I'm here to tell you that you *can* be classy and fabulous, and that mean ol' Coco Chanel can't hurt you anymore because she's dead. Like, *super* dead.[*] And while that's certainly good news, the bad news is that becoming a classy and fabulous man is a lot harder for men than it is for women. It's just another one of those fundamental unfairnesses our gender has to deal with.

That's right, I'm coming out here and now and saying it—I love fashion. Anyone who's ever met me will attest that my overall sense of style rivals that of today's most success-

---

[*] Like, died-in-1971 dead.

ful and flamboyant fashionistas. (Yeah, I'm talking to you, Dennis Rodman!)*

Now, look, before we get started, a word of encouragement. Don't beat yourself up about how you do on this quiz. It's unrealistic to think you're going to get anywhere close to where I am stylistically. That doesn't mean you shouldn't try. Learning where the gaps are in your fashion education is the only way to improve. Plus, if you have even a shred of class and style going on, chances are you'll do better at this than Mac, Charlie, or Frank.

YOUR FASHION SENSE:

HOW BAD IS IT?

1. What are you most likely to use to keep warm when it's a little chilly?
    1. A cardigan.
    2. A hoodie.
    3. A bottle of whiskey.
    4. Wolf pelt.

2. What's your favorite color?
    1. Red.
    2. White.

---

* Just kidding. Dennis Rodman dresses like a dick.

3. Black.

4. Beyoncé.

3. A jacquard is . . .

    1. a type of weaving.

    2. something that sounds vaguely French.

    3. the captain of the USS *Enterprise*.

    4. what I do when I need to get off really quickly.

4. Spatterdashes are . . .

    1. shoes.

    2. a footwear accessory used to cover the ankle.

    3. something Elton John does to his favorite roadies.

    4. what comes out when I jacquard.

5. Who is your style icon?

    1. George Clooney.

    2. Jay Z.

    3. Cher.

    4. Dennis Reynolds.

    5. Dennis Reynolds.

    6. 1, 4, and 5.

6. Whenever you pass a mirror you . . .

    1. stop and check yourself out.

    2. take time out for a quick bump.

    3. stop and check to see if you've been turned
into a vampire.

4. ask it questions about how good-looking it thinks
   you are.

7. What is your favorite material?
   1. Tweed.
   2. Cotton.
   3. Wool.
   4. Silk.
   5. Skin.

8. Of the following well-known anti-Semites, who would
you say is/was the most fashionable?
   1. John Galliano.
   2. Coco Chanel.
   3. Adolf Hitler.
   4. Mel Gibson.

9. Which best describes your hairstyle?
   1. Marc Singer.
   2. Hulk Hogan.
   3. Jesse Ventura.
   4. John Travolta.

10. How much pubic hair should the classy man have?
   1. All of it.
   2. Most of it.
   3. Trimmed on a 1.
   4. Laser-beamed off.

11. Accessories are . . .
    1. key for bringing the whole fashion package together.
    2. easy to steal from other people's dressers.
    3. something you can trade for crack in a pinch.
    4. a good place to hide your blow.

12. Which of the following supermodels would you most like to watch me bang?
    1. Cheryl Tiegs on the cover of the 1975 *Sports Illustrated* Swimsuit Issue (before she got wrinkly).
    2. Kate Moss (before she got fat).
    3. Kate Upton (turned upside down-ton).
    4. Tom Brady (because, shit, *Tom Brady!*).

13. The most awesome song to listen to at full blast while you're trying on different outfits in front of the mirror before a big night out scoring chicks is . . .
    1. "Man in the Mirror" by Michael Jackson.
    2. "Higher Love" by Steve Winwood.
    3. "I'm Too Sexy" by those bald European dudes.
    4. "Never Gonna Give You Up" by Rick Astley.
    5. "I Touch Myself" by the Divinyls.
    6. "You Sexy Thing" by Hot Chocolate.
    7. "Hurt" by Nine Inch Nails.
    8. My super-mega mashup of all of those songs.

Answer key:

Add up the corresponding number next to each answer chosen. If the total is . . .

Less than 10: You have the fashion sense of a McPoyle.

Between 10 and 18: You have potential: the potential to be publicly mocked.

18 or 19: You are Charlie.

Exactly 19: Congratulations! You're eligible for our grand-prize drawing!

Between 20 and 24: If you were a chick I'd bang you but then never call.

25 or above: You passed the quiz. But, you know, so what?

PART IV

Health and Diet

All-Time Top

Physiques

By Mac

W hen it comes to ultimate success in life, few things will get you there faster than building and maintaining a powerhouse physique. I wanted to take a moment to name those things. The first thing that will get you there faster is being born rich. That helps out like crazy. Same with having some kind of superhuman ability, like X-ray vision or shape-shifting. If you can do any of that stuff, going to the gym is a waste of your time. You can just shape-shift into a muscle-bound hulk any time you need to. Or maybe time travel is your superpower. If so, you can just go back in time and buy a bunch of Microsoft stock or direct *Avatar* or something. And then with all that money you can buy everything you need to be happy, including people to tell you you're ripped, no matter how fat you are.

In most cases, though, you've got to earn success the old-fashioned way—in the gym, one squat, one dead lift, one butt crunch at a time. Just ask Jesse Ventura, whose sinewy frame was so perfect that in his heyday they gave him the nickname "the Body." Think about that for a second. That's like being so smart that people call you "the Brain," or so cool that everyone calls you "the Fonz."

But Jesse Ventura didn't just sit around getting his pump on, oiling himself up, and showing off his vascular pecs and taut glutes. He used that ripped bod to get ahead. First he got ahead as a wrestling champion, then he got ahead as a Hollywood leading man. After that he became governor of an actual U.S. state. And now he's one of the country's leading experts on the conspiracy to cover up the Reptile People, the conspiracy to cover up the Soviet Union's death ray, and the conspiracy to keep Pauly Shore from working in Hollywood anymore. A conspiracy that I would be on the board of if there were such a thing. The Weasel? Fuck off.

But you get my point. Jesse "the Body" Ventura has used his *mass* to gain *mass appeal*. Oh bam! You like that wordplay? No? Screw you then. You don't deserve a good body. Learn what good wordplay is first.

But anyway, my point is, Jesse Ventura's not the only famous guy who flexed his muscles in order to become a dominant force on the battlefield that is his life. Here are some of the heroes I myself try to emulate:

Carl Weathers

He's obviously most famous for his role as George Dillon in the greatest action movie ever made (do I even need to say it? Seriously? Here's a hint: "If it bleeds, we can kill it"), but Mr. Weathers has also delivered standout performances in several other kick-ass motion pictures including *Force 10 from Navarone; Hurricane Smith; Action Jackson;* the three best boxing movies ever, *Rockys I, II,* and *III;* the second-most hilarious Adam Sandler comedy of all time, *Little Nicky* (number one will always be *Billy Madison*); and *Shadow Warriors 2: Hunt for the Death Merchant* (which I haven't seen yet but am having specially imported from Vietnam). With his broad shoulders and burly chest, Mr. Weathers's ebony, ebony body has been showcased shirtless—by my count—in all but three of his films. This count does not include *Shadow Warriors 2: Hunt for the Death Merchant*, which, again, I haven't seen yet, but I will get back to you on that with full notes when I do. In addition to being a movie star, Mr. Weathers also played professional football, served on the United States Olympic Committee, and judging from the number of times he's been married (three), banged a lot of women.

Brian Bosworth

Just as his promising pro football career was cut short by a horrific injury, the Boz's film career also ended before its time due to a devastating lack of interest. What can I say? People are stupid. Because the truth of the matter is the Boz had serious acting chops, and *Stone Cold* is a goddamn masterpiece. As fine a meditation on crime and punishment as that famous book by that Russian dude. I forget what it's called. What separated the Boz from his contemporaries was his core strength. I mean, go back and look at pictures and you'll see that his obliques alone could crush a man's nuts. Having those kinds of rippling quick-twitch core muscles helps an actor react faster and stronger, and lets his body distribute stress evenly and absorb shock effectively. That's why if I'm making a movie, I'd take the Boz over Dustin Hoffman any day.

Arnold Alois Schwarzenegger

Jesus, where do I even begin? Four-time Mr. Universe? Seven-time Mr. Olympia? Banging a Kennedy? *The Terminator*? The Governator? *True Lies*? Knocking up his housekeeper and keeping it a secret for *thirteen years*? From a Kennedy? *Predator*? *Conan the Barbarian*? That movie where the weird-looking little guy played his twin brother? Being so awesomely ripped that he made people forget that his dad was a Nazi? Squatting 545 pounds? No, seriously, tell me—where do I even possibly begin with this great, hulking mass of a man? The only way I know to avoid starting is to finish.

Dolph Lundgren

Fact: Dolph Lundgren is universally recognized as one of the greatest action stars of all time.

Fact: At six foot five and two hundred fifty pounds of pure physical magnificence, Dolph is the most intimidating screen presence since Godzilla. And a slightly better actor.

Fact: Dolph is from Sweden, a country that also produced *True Blood* star Alexander Skarsgård. Let the record show that Alexander Skarsgård is also extremely ripped.

Fact: Dolph is a third-degree black belt who won the European championship in 1980 and '81.

Fact: Dolph's got a master's degree in chemistry or some shit.

Fact: Dolph banged Grace Jones and lived to tell about it.

Fact: Dolph is so badass, Charlie and I wrote a movie for him to star in called *The Fifth Sense* in which Dolph plays a scientist who wears a mesh shirt and has doglike senses so he can smell crime before it happens. It's pretty awesome. Call me, Dolph!

Fact: "I must break you" is the fifth-greatest movie quote ever. Which reminds me, this is the perfect spot to put my list of the top ten greatest movie quotes ever. Editor person, can you please add this list in here somewhere?*

* EDITOR'S NOTE: Sure. At this point, if it's words, in some approximation of English, I'll take it. Just yesterday Mr. Kelly tried to submit grainy video footage from inside a heating duct as a "chapter."

THE TOP 10 GREATEST MOVIE QUOTES EVER

10. **"I don't step on toes . . . I step on necks."**
—James Braddock (Chuck Norris) in *Braddock: Missing in Action 30*[*]

9. **"Always bet on black."**
—John Cutter (Wesley Snipes) in *Passenger 57*[†]

8. **"You're a disease, and I'm the cure."**
—Marion "Cobra" Cobretti (Sylvester Stallone) in *Cobra*

7. **"I'm too old for this shit!"**
—Roger Murtaugh (Danny Glover) in every *Lethal Weapon* movie now and forever

6. **"He's got a real pretty mouth, ain't he?"**
—Toothless Man (Herbert "Cowboy" Coward) in *Deliverance*

5. **"I must break you."**
—Ivan Drago (Dolph Lundgren) in *Rocky IV*[‡]

4. **"If it bleeds, we can kill it."**
—Alan "Dutch" Schaefer (Arnold Schwarzenegger) in *Predator*

3. **"Bleed, bastard!"**
—Alan "Dutch" Schaefer (Arnold Schwarzenegger) in *Predator*

2. **"I ain't got time to bleed."**
—Blain Cooper (Jesse Ventura) in *Predator*

1. **"Come on . . . Come on! Do it! Do it! Come on. Come on! Kill me! I'm here! Kill me! I'm here! Kill me! Come on! Kill me! I'm here! Come on! Do it now! Kill me!"**
—Alan "Dutch" Schaefer (Arnold Schwarzenegger) in *Predator*

---

[*] When properly executed, a Chuck Norris neck-stepping is impossible to defend against.

[†] Especially true when your only other betting option is red. I mean, think about it. You bet on red, who do you get? The Indian from those littering commercials? Lou Diamond Phillips? Come on!

[‡] See, what'd I tell you?

Bruce Lee

Who says all Asian guys are short and have little dicks? (Lots of people, actually. Especially in my neighborhood.) But there is one Asian guy who even the most hard-core racist would never say that about, and that's Bruce Lee. In fact, there's this dude named Russ White who was in jail with my dad who's a card-carrying member of the Aryan Brotherhood and, get this, Bruce Lee is his favorite actor of all time. And not just because Bruce kicked the shit out of Kareem Abdul-Jabbar in *Game of Death* either. (And man, does Russ White ever hate Kareem Abdul-Jabbar. Not so much because he's black as because he was on the Lakers when they beat the Sixers for the championship in 1980. Although the being-black thing probably doesn't help.) Point is, dead or alive, Bruce Lee kicks ass and even asshole racists like Russ White understand that.

Sylvester Stallone

If you want to make it in Hollywood as a giant muscle-bound hardass, it helps if no one can understand what you're saying. Most guys do this by coming from a weird place with a weird accent and not bothering to learn to speak English good. Only Stallone had the balls to be born and raised in the US of A and *still* be completely unintelligible. You can't do that without immense reserves of talent and a body-fat percentage in the low single digits. Plus, I've got a soft spot for actor/director/writer/producers who hail from Philly. As the actor/director/writer/producer of *Lethal Weapon 5* and *6* I know how hard it is to be a creative genius stuck in a body so gorgeous nobody takes you seriously. I'm more than just a slab of beef, people.

Jason Statham

Like I've told Dennis numerous times, Statham is a total badass. I'm not saying his physique has anything on the lineup in *Predator*, but at this stage in the game, he probably has tighter abs and firmer thighs than Arnold or Carl Weathers. But that's just because he's younger. It remains to be seen how his body will handle the test of time. Believe me, I'll be keeping track. Before becoming an actor, Statham was a member of Britain's National Diving Squad for twelve years. Then he dove into being one of the best modern action film stars into the universe. Again . . . wordplay, boom.

Tim Tebow

This one almost goes without saying. I mean, first off his mom flat-out *refused* to abort him. If that's not love, I don't know what is. Tim Tebow is like Jesus, Mary, and Joseph all rolled into one. He's got those generous, feminine features, but you can tell that underneath his clothes he's all man. And I'm pretty sure he turned water into wine this one game. That's what "Tebowing" is, right? I don't really watch the Broncos. Anyway, would someone please cast him in a movie already? With a little Hollywood juice, this guy could be the next Brian Bosworth. Plus he loves the shit out of God.

Jean-Claude Van Damme

I got just two words for you. *Bloodsport*. You wouldn't think a white man, let alone a Belgian, could plausibly pull off being a highly trained Ninjitsu master, but it's just another day at the office for the Muscles from Brussels. The pure awesomeness of this movie aside, though, I always found Ninjitsu a little fruity. "Oooh, look at me, I'm sneaking around in the shadows with my little *shuriken*s. Actually don't look at me, 'cause I'm a *ninja*."

Sneaky little jerks. I prefer to do my karate katas in the middle of a well-lit room so everyone can see my sweet-ass moves. But Ninjitsu or no Ninjitsu, I gotta kneel to a man who can execute a helicopter-style jump-spinning heel kick like that. The rest of the JCVD flicks are pretty sweet too. My second favorite has to be *Hard Target,* which, it turns out, is not the name of a porn. Wait, Dennis told me he has a porn movie with that name. Okay, so fine, it's both.

Wolverine

I hate comic-book movies. Screw mutants and men in capes using CGI special effects to trick my eyes into thinking they're badasses. That's why all the dudes on my list could totally be in the next *Expendables,* except for Bruce Lee, may he rest in everlasting peace. But there is one exception to my comic-book hate: Wolverine. The name's badass and the dude is a straight-up beefcake. I mean Wolverine in 2000 was sick, but dude is seriously getting more and more diesel. I saw him in this *Australia* movie, pouring water all over himself with Nicole Kidman and shit. Beefcake city. Traps and lats, traps and lats. Respect.

28

Recipe Corner:
RUM HAM

By Frank

I used to buy my hams prerummed, but that was before I realized I could make my own quickly, easily, and just about anywhere.

INGREDIENTS

1 10-pound canned ham

1 hunting knife

3 1-liter bottles of rum

1 handgun

1 box handgun ammo

1 bunch of Italian parsley

When choosing a rum for this recipe, just go with the cheapest one they got down at the state store. Some snobs out there might disagree with me on this, but I'm telling ya, there ain't no point blowing a lot of dough on that fancy shit from some island you can't even pronounce because in the end, you're not even gonna taste the rum. If you do, it means you did the rumming wrong. All you're supposed to be tasting is a greasy cooked pig that smells like it was out getting blitzed all night at Tomiko's Tiki Bar. Plus, with the money you save buying cheap rum, you can buy condoms to bang Tomiko. Because trust me, you DO NOT want to bang Tomiko without a condom. (Set a little money aside to settle up with her afterward, too. She's not the sort to let you run a tab.)

You can use any kind of ham you want, but I personally lean toward an Irish ham cuz those crafty micks brine that pink gold to perfection. That means all you gotta do is chase out the brine with booze and you're set. Make sure it's a precooked canned jobbie too. They travel much easier, and you don't have to worry about getting the shits if you don't cook it right.

Finally, there's choosing your gun. I go with a Smith & Wesson Model 19 snub-nose. So far that's been more than enough firepower to keep hungry drunks away from my rum ham. Especially if I'm planning on eating it under the bridge.

DIRECTIONS

1. De-can ham (for instructions, see back of can).
2. Using the hunting knife, carve a hole in the top of the ham wide enough to hold the mouth of a rum bottle.
3. Open first rum bottle and upend it into your ham hole. If you made your hole deep enough, it should stand up there on its own.
4. Load gun.

5. Open second rum bottle and upend it into your ham hole (the one in your face this time). As the liquid flows into your mouth, swallow at regular intervals.

6. Repeat step five until bottle is empty.

7. Open third bottle of rum and repeat step six.

8. Remove safety from handgun.

9. Wait for ham pirates.

10. Shoot ham pirates.

11. Reload gun.

12. Repeat steps eight through eleven until rum has been fully absorbed into ham, usually about twelve hours.

13. Garnish with parsley and serve.

29

Imagining a
New You

By Dennis

Hello, sad self-help-book-buying friend. It's your old pal Dennis here with a little exercise for you to try. Now, I know what you're saying. "Dennis, I've tried the exercises! I've done the trust falls, I've made amends with my spirit animal, I've gone to my high school girlfriend's house and stood there in a trench coat with a boom box held over my head blasting the Best Song in the World.* And none of it has worked. I'm still fat, lazy, and, oh dear Christ, am I ugly."

Well first off, easy on the words there, fatty, I don't have all day for you to vent about your problems. Who's writing this book anyway? Certainly not you. In fact, quite to the contrary—I see you skulking around in the self-help section looking for the book (written by ME) that will finally fix you once and for all.

---

* Lionel Richie's "Hello."

But listen, listen, easy there. It's just a little tough love from big D over here. Little truth bomb. And the truth is, you don't need a giant overhaul (except maybe in your musical taste[*]). I mean, on the ugly scale you're a three at best. Which, when you think about it, is not that ugly at all. Mac, for instance, is also a three in ugly, so even if this exercise we're going to try fails, you'll have some company at your ugly parties (they still have those, right?). For the record, on the ugly scale Charlie is a five, Frank is a six, and Dee is a nine.

Now, I know that might seem harsh on my sister, given the fact that she's almost definitely going to read the book we're cowriting and be deeply hurt by what I just said.[†] But you should keep a couple things in mind. First off, I really, *really* like being mean to her. Secondly, until she starts living in reality, she's never going to improve herself. Not that I particularly want her to improve herself, mind you. See, now that my friends and I are in the life-fixing game, we are going to be making tall dollars on the seminar circuit. And to do that, we are going to need someone around to be the cautionary tale.

But I digress. I said we'd try a little exercise here for you and I'll be good and goddamned if we don't. And this exercise is guaranteed to make you feel better, look better, and smell better in mere minutes, without costing you any more than you have already paid for this book with your sad, lonely dollars. This exercise is what we in the fixin'-folk biz like to call a "visuality." That's a cross between a visualization and a reality. Now, as you probably know, a visualization is just some bullshit someone makes up to help you feel better. But when you mix it with a REALITY? When you create a VISUALITY? I'm telling you, you do that, and there is no limit to the bullshit you can bring into the world.

---

[*] The best song in the world is Lionel Richie's "Dancing on the Ceiling," you poor sap.

[†] EDITOR'S NOTE: I sincerely doubt the former, and the latter.

So let's get started. Find a comfortable chair. Take a moment to center yourself. Now draw in a deep breath and close your eyes. Dark, huh? And scary. You don't know who might be in here with you, do you? Well surprise, surprise, cowboy. It's me. And we have a few things to talk about, pardner. Seems you haven't been exactly up-front with me here. See, I distinctly remember telling you to close your eyes. And yet, you're still here, supposedly still "reading" my book even though you have your eyes closed. Well, which is it, Kreskin? You got your eyes closed or are you reading? Either you disobeyed me or you disrespected me. Either way, we got unfinished business. Uncooked beef, you might say. Wouldn't want someone to wake up with a nasty case of *E. coli*, now, would we? That's what I thought. Let's keep the ego in check from here on out, okay? OKAY.

Now, I'm going to try to put all that unpleasantness behind us and do this visuality with you, but I gotta be honest, it's throwing off my game a little. But I suppose this is the kind of behavior that led you to the self-help section in the first place with your bad skin and hollow eyes and basic lack of purpose. But you know what? I'm bigger than that. I'm not going to let your failings be the things that hold you back. We're doing this visuality and then we're doing some shots, after which I'm going to find some young nubile thing to bed. Without you. No offense, but you're not exactly wingman material.

OKAY, so let's get this over with then. Close your eyes and imagine that you are no longer the sad, lonely fatty you that you've been your entire life, but rather a far superior version of you that is less sad, less lonely, and less fat. Small children and dogs do *not* cower when they see you coming. In fact, not only are you not sad, lonely, and fat, you are suave, good-looking, smart, charming, and hanging a ton of dong. If you're finding this difficult to visualize, you're not alone. Most people find it nearly impossible to see themselves as anything but giant losers. Pretty understandable, given the fact that most people actually *are* giant losers. It can be tough. The key thing to remember is you're not like them. You only *look* like a loser. Inside you lurks a winner, a shady sort

144

of creepy winner who owns three windowless vans and never talks to the neighbors.

You know what? Forget what I said about you being a winner inside. I may have . . . *exaggerated* slightly. We've got more work to do here than I thought. And we need to be realistic. Scratch actually *becoming* a winner off your to-do list. Our top priority right now is having you *believe* you're a winner, no matter what the truth might be.

No problem. We're just going to have to turn this visuality into a "hypnality." That's where I do a little light hypnosis and convince you to believe whatever I think is best for you. (I use a form of this when I go on dates, actually, but today we're going to skip the part where I roofie your drink.) You, my friend, are on a vision quest. And unlike those bullshit "walkabout" trips where you go into the outback with no food or water and only a knife for protection, on this vision quest you are guaranteed to see a vision.

So clear your mind (you can keep your eyes open this time; maybe we can ease up on our lie quotient while we're at it) and focus on the clarity of your perception of the next image, nay, the next VISION you will see. It is a man, but it is also so much more than a man. His body is sculpted to the proportions of Michelangelo's *David*. His radiant hair rests upon an exquisitely shaped skull like a crown forged from the solid-gold balls of Zeus himself. And those soulful penetrating eyes, don't get me started on the soulful penetrating eyes. When you turn the page, you will see this vision. Soak him in, in all his luxuriant marvelousness, and imagine that that chiseled exemplar of human perfection is you. And now, I give you the greatest gift of all (apart from all the amazing words you just read that I wrote for you) . . .

Welcome to your new you. Me.

30

Recipe Corner:

BLUE TEA À LA CHARLIE

By Charlie and Frank

Hey, it's Frank. I'm going to take the writing duties on this one and let Charlie do what he does best: create culinary masterpieces. He wanted to make sure I passed along the recipe for one of our favorite relaxing beverages, Blue Tea. Stuff goes dynamite with cat food. Now, I should warn you, it takes all evening to make up a batch, but once you do, you'll have IBT (Iced Blue Tea) in the fridge for weeks. Plus, sometimes it's nice just to sit home cooking on a cold night.

INGREDIENTS

1 cup olive oil

1 industrial-size stockpot

3 or 4 pairs of jeans, any size (if you
don't have any lying around, check down
under the bridge)

10 to 12 gallons of water

5 Delaware River sewage runoff crabs

1 star anise

lemon wedges

sugar to taste

DIRECTIONS

Add oil to the stockpot and turn heat to high. Once the oil is hot enough, toss in all your denim and sauté it for 5 to 10 minutes. Don't move it around too much, you want to get a good sear going. Once the denim starts to smoke, pour in the water (make sure the denim is completely covered) and add the crabs and star anise. Bring to a boil, then reduce heat to a simmer. Simmer for 6 hours, stirring often, until the crabs have completely disintegrated. The water should now be a milky blue. Strain into a container and let cool. Serve with a lemon wedge and sugar as desired. Don't drink it all at once!

31

EDITOR'S NOTE: For the record, despite my numerous entreaties to Messrs. Reynolds, Kelly, and McDonald, I was repeatedly denied access to Ms. Reynolds and was unable to communicate with her about this book directly. After receiving her piece on looking like a bird, I became worried that she'd suffered some sort of catastrophic break from reality. However, I've since learned that she was given several so-called assignments attributed to a fictional male editor at Titan Books named Damon Nightman. We now believe these assignments originated with Messrs. Reynolds, Kelly, and McDonald. One of Ms. Reynolds's responses to these assignments follows.

Aluminum Humor

By Dee

Okay, so what is the deal here? The guys have pretty much written about whatever the hell they want to for this stupid book, but dipshit Damon (yeah, I said it, Damon) keeps giving me these bottom-

149

of-the-barrel assignments. And it's weird because you seemed really cool at first. The in-depth exposé on the trials and tribulations of being an actress? Right up my alley. Something I could really sink my teeth into. And, boom, I nailed it! After that I figured you'd be kissing my ass. Maybe even take me out on the town for some wining and dining on the Titan Books expense account. And after dinner, well, who knows? Maybe I'd let the editor come back to my place to dot my i's and cross my t's, if you get what I'm saying.*

But then what do you do? You turn around and ask me to write some ridiculous nonsense about how to look like a bird. How the hell is that helping anyone? Oh, and now you have the balls to assign me an article on aluminum humor. *Aluminum humor?* Seriously, shithead?! I don't even know what the hell that is.

I'm a pro, though. I understand that part of becoming a great author is honing your ability to write about bullshit you don't know anything about and making it seem like you do. And hell, if Malcolm Gladwell can do it, so can I. So I Googled "aluminum humor." And I came up with a few things.

What do you call a one-inch-by-three-inch strip of aluminum that sticks on one side?

A Band-Aid for the Tin Man!

Okay, not starting off so strong. Thanks a lot, Internet. Let's see, oh, here's another one.

What did Dick Dastardly say when he crashed his car into a sheet of aluminum?

"Curses, foiled again."

Jesus, I don't know how Gladwell puts up with this kind of crap. Okay, one more.

Gold and Aluminum meet up and Gold says, "What's up, Al?" Then Gold runs off all of a sudden, so Aluminum shouts "A U!"

---

* What I'm saying is, is that we'd bone.

I found that one in *The Periodic Guide to Humor.* Goddamn I hate nerds, but you probably love nerd jokes, huh, Damon?

Listen, I think we can still work together, but you assigning me topics like this just isn't working out, nerd. This is a self-help book and I know how to help myself better than anyone I know. So from here on I'm just going to write whatever I feel like and you can let me know later what a genius I am. I'm glad we had this talk.

32

Hey, Frank here. Charlie got all freaked out the other day about how everyone was writing all their parts for the book and he didn't have as many and they were all gonna be rich and famous writers and he'd be stuck doing their Charlie Work forever. Anyway, long story short, he begged me to help him write a chapter of this thing. He said he wanted the book to be classy and he was just the guy to bring the atmosphere up a notch with some writing about cheese. Nothing more classy than cheese. Honestly I have no idea if he succeeded. I've been trying to forget everything I ever learned about class. It's going pretty good so far.

Recipe Corner:

CHARLIE'S CHEESE RECIPES

By Charlie (as told to Frank)

The traditional way to make cheese is, of course, to milk a bird and then let it ferment in your fridge. (The milk, not the bird. Keep the rest of the bird in the freezer 'til you're ready to use it.) But who has time for that, what with all the instability and the lies? World leaders, am I right? Anyway, I'm a man who likes cheese and I can't be at the whim of politicians all the time. Here's how I like to make cheese.

RECIPE #1

This one is rock solid. The most reliable cheese recipe I know of. A little expensive, but if you can afford this fancy "book" then you can afford this. Order a large extra-cheese pizza. Ask them to hold the dough and the sauce. Boom. You just made cheese.

RECIPE #2

This recipe yields slightly less cheese but has the advantage of being absolutely, 100 percent free. Simply round up all the rat traps in the basement. You will notice that each one has a small piece of cheese attached to it. Remove all cheese pieces to a plate and press together. Boom. You just made cheese.

RECIPE #3

~~~~~~~

This recipe is somewhat unpredictable, but it's cheap and when it works you end up with enough cheese to last you for weeks. In a jug, combine two cups orange juice with two cups heavy cream. Add a teaspoon of salt and two tablespoons of baking powder and shake vigorously. Now leave in a cool, quiet place. Back in the olden days they used to leave their cheeses in a cave, but I find the spot behind the last toilet in the ladies' room works really well. (Note: Don't use the men's room, the smell will cause complaints.) Wait two weeks. Boom. You just made cheese. The black stuff on top is supposed to be there, that's what cheeserians (the fraternal brotherhood of cheese makers) call "crud." Just stir it in and enjoy on crackers or simply by itself! Purists may give you a hard time about this recipe. I've even had people tell me that it isn't cheese at all (hey, haters gon' hate). But nothing silences a roomful of haters like shoveling a giant spoonful into your mouth. Most of the time, they just stop what they're doing and walk away.

33

Recipe Corner:

CHICKEN SOUP FOR THE 'HOLE

By Dee

INGREDIENTS

1 asshole who won't leave your apartment

1 can chicken soup

About 10 cans' worth of water

T his one's for the ladies out there. You know who I'm talkin' 'bout! Let's hear it for the ones with the boobies and the lumps and the "hey let's get me sumps." (Did I just make up a cool new term? Go ahead and use "sumps" if you ladies want, but make sure you give me credit, because it's pretty awesome and I don't want any dumb bitches stealing my awesome catchwords.) Okay, are all the men gone? Good, because I'm about to let you in on one of Sweet Dee's little secrets.

You know what tastes good on a cold winter's night when some jerkoff booty call can't take a hint that it's time to leave already? A little thing I like to call Chicken Soup for the 'Hole. Because the night started out fine, didn't it? He bought you White Castle and didn't make you go see that new romcom about the blind girl and the deaf dog and the borderline-retarded dreamboat who falls in love with her. And then you end up back at your place, which is where you wanted to go all along, only stupid White Castle doesn't deliver and it just happens to be around the corner from the movie place, but hey, you fake a little food poisoning and bingo! No spending an hour and a half watching Ryan Reynolds try to cry, no having to back up your claim that he's your estranged brother, no having to kiss his goddamn stupid lips every time he starts feeling romantic and reaches over the armrest. Plus, you just ate White Castle, so no one's going to doubt your story.

Anyway, so you get back to your place, you make a miraculous re-covery just in time for some bangin' (finally), and then the little shitstain won't leave. Never fear, ladies, I have a foolproof method for removing even the most stubborn shitstain from your apartment.

Making a fast break is key. Within a minute of getting your cook-ies, jump up and insist you make him soup. Tell him you always cook for your studs and, what the hell, you'll cook for him too. Get your can of soup and try to open it. The key here is *try*. Under no circumstances should you succeed. Call him from the kitchen using a sweet, seductive tone: "Oh, lover! Could you come in here a minute?" When he does, put on your best widdle-girl-in-a-big-world helpless face and hold out the can opener as you say, "I need a big stwong man to work this compwicated machine." Moan softly every time he twists the lever and say, "My daddy used to open all the cans in our house."

This on its own is often enough to clear out all but the biggest dirtdogs.

If he persists in hanging around, it's time to turn up the heat. Which is to say, turn on one of your stove's burners, but don't light it. Sometimes it takes guys a while to notice this one, so be prepared to breathe a little gas. I usually practice breathing gas for a while right before I go out to build up my tolerance a bit. One of two outcomes here. First, he doesn't notice, the room fills with gas, and he passes out (now who's the dummy, non–gas breathers?). This one's easy. Shut off the gas and try not to make any sparks as you drag his unconscious ass out into the hall. Pin a note to his chest that says, "Syphilis," and with any luck you'll never hear from him again.

The second outcome, though, of course is that he shuts off the gas and helps you properly light the stove. You should pretend like this is the most amazing thing you've ever seen. Let your eyes be filled with childlike wonder. Reach out toward the flame as though it's the most beautiful thing you have ever seen. Tell him, "You brought the blue angels. I love dancing with the blue angels." Get out a saucepan and dump in the contents of the can. Now start filling the can with water and dumping it into the saucepan. As you do this, begin softly singing to yourself the following ditty:

> *Mama's gone across the sea*
> *Daddy's here, just him and me*
> *Before the men with animal masks*
> *Come make me do their awful tasks*

Keep singing and keep dumping cans of water into the pan until it overflows. If he is not gone by now, begin plotting an escape route. You have brought home a raging psychopath. Again.

34

Recipe Corner:
RACCOON
STEAK

By Frank

B ack when I was in 'Nam I had to do a lot of things I didn't want to in order to survive. I'm talking some really horrible shit. Most of it involved women, but not always. These days the Third World is all one big giant vacation resort. But when I was there, Southeast Asia was completely insane, full of whores, and factory workers, and whores. But a lot's changed since the nineties. Except the whore bit. That remains.

One of the handiest things I learned back then, back when I was doing whatever it took to survive, is that cooked coon flesh tastes almost identical to cooked people flesh. I don't want to get into exactly how I came into this knowledge. Let's just say I know a guy. Or rather I knew a guy. A real sweetheart and good to have with you in a pinch. Little stringy though. What I'm saying is, the fact that coon meat tastes like human meat is good from a flavor standpoint, but as most of us know, it isn't best to eat other humans. 1) You can get very sick from it. 2) Unless you have some weird psychological craving to masticate and ingest your fellow man, the guilt you feel will likely cancel out the enjoyable flavor of the meat. 3) While I'm sure some of you could justify it, eating human flesh is generally frowned upon and highly illegal. That said, if you do decide to eat a person, try eating a vegan. Those assholes deserve to be eaten and they taste the best. Notice how most carnivores eat herbivores. See where I'm going with this? But I digress.

When it comes to the flavor, coon meat is blander than human, but with a little salt and paprika—bam—you may as well be munching on your closest enemy (insert enemy name here. Mine's name is Alan). I swear, you cook coon meat right and not even the most discerning palate can tell the difference. Just ask my old drinking buddy Anthony Bourdain what happened the last time we got blackout drunk at my buddy Fong's restaurant in Chinatown. On second thought, don't ask him. To this day, he still has no idea I pulled the old coon switcheroo on him.

Raccoon steak can also come in handy if you wanna get a tapeworm to lose some weight. The stuff is lousy with parasites. If you're going the tapeworm route, you'll want to prepare your coon meat rare. You get a good solid tapeworm to set up shop in your stomach, and within three weeks you'll have dropped thirty pounds.

INGREDIENTS

~~~~~~

1 medium raccoon

2 tablespoons salt

1 tablespoon paprika

an unstoppable hunger for human flesh

DIRECTIONS

~~~~~~~~

1. Get a racoon.

Shooting a live one ensures it's good and fresh, but that ain't legal in most cities.* Plus, raccoons tend to hang around Dumpsters, which means there's always a chance of a stray bullet hittin' some homeless asshole, and the meat on those guys tastes terrible (not enough greens, know what I mean?). A roadkill raccoon is free and you don't need to use a gun, but be careful. Ever since the economy went to shit and they cut the highway cleanup budgets, sometimes roadkill lays out there for weeks on end. Ideally you want to go run one over yourself, so you know it's halfway fresh.

2. De-fur the raccoon.

If you have time, skinning it is the best method because when you're done you got yourself a beautiful pelt you can use for anything. Everyone knows they make great hats, but if you ask me, nothing beats a pair of coonskin socks. They feel great on your toes, they look stylish, and they're surprisingly sweat-absorbent. But sometimes you're in a hurry and you don't got time for skinning. If you want to go the fast route, just douse the little guy in gasoline and light him up. Smells pretty bad for a second, but if you do it right, you melt the fur and skin right off and you can give your steaks a nice presear.

---

* Thanks a lot, Obama.

3. Field-dress the raccoon.

I always make Charlie do this part because his clothes usually have a lot of blood on them anyway. Basically you want to get the thing's digestive tract out of there. The stomach, the intestines, and the shitter all gotta come out. You don't want that in with your steaks. They're better for making soup with.

4. Chop off its head.

You don't need to do this, but it's a lot of fun. Charlie and I always flip a coin to decide who gets to do it. That way it's fair.

5. Harvest your steaks.

This is a lot more difficult than lopping off the thing's head. Raccoons are solid meat inside and it takes a lot of hacking to get through it. The steaks we make aren't always the prettiest, but I'm telling you, pretty don't matter to your mouth.

6. Dry-rub.

I use a two-to-one salt-paprika mix. When in doubt, use extra dry-rub!

7. Grill.

Raccoon tastes best when cooked over an open flame. Best way is over a trash can fire, but if you get jammed up, you can just do it on Charlie's radiator. Don't cook it too long, though, no more than two minutes on a side. Remember, we want to preserve as much of that raccoony flavor as possible. Plus when you cook it too long you kill all the parasites. A well-done coon steak is a waste of a good tapeworm.

8. Serve.

Raccoon is a little gamey. Kind of like rabbit but dirtier. It pairs very well with rubbing alcohol, but you have to be careful with that too. Too much rubbing alcohol will kill your tapeworm before it has a chance to really get going. If Charlie and I are feeling flush, we'll cook up some eggs along with the steaks. Just make sure the crows are gone before you go grab 'em. Those bastards are mean sonofabitches when they're pissed off.

35

Spiritual

Nutrition

By Mac

L et me tell you something, people. I've learned a thing or two about what it takes to pack on mass and build the perfect body. It starts with nutrition, but not that food-pyramid high-protein no-smoking crap. I'm talking about spiritual nutrition here. Because when you eat right, God notices. And when God notices, He reaches down and boom, He drops a little Mr. Universe on you.

See, in the beginning, God created Adam and Eve. But to spice things up a little He also created apple trees (God's not a big partier). Now, God's sole purpose in creating these apple trees was to decorate the Garden of Eden. Class it up a little. Once God had the trees arranged perfectly—and I mean perfectly, this is God we're talking about—God flat-out forbored Adam and Eve from eating the fruit the trees bade. Because, Jesus Christ, He had that shit arranged PERFECTLY. You can't just go around eating perfection. On the plus side, He told them it was totally cool for them to be totally naked in public all the time.

Well clearly Adam and Eve didn't give two shits about landscape design, perfection, or God's Plan for Us All. They were all, "Oh hey, what's this apple, maybe I shouldn't eat it like God said, oh wait no, I don't give a shit." They start eating the frickin' decorations. God's decorations. Then, when God's all, "What the fuck are you doing to my apples? I told you those were off-limits," they tried to blame it on a serpent. *Really*, Adam and Eve? You think God Almighty, maker of all things living, isn't aware of the fact that serpents are carnivores and live in the sea? When was the last time you saw a serpent in a *garden*? Did you think that in His rush to get the whole world finished in a week (which, by the way, He nailed in just six days) that He'd forget about the dietary habits, seafaring predilections, and general improbability of serpents? I think not. God doesn't forget shit. He's like an elephant, only way, way bigger.

And God can't just let this slide. I mean come on. So check out what He does. First He casts them out of the Garden of Eden. Then He hits them with the capacity to feel shame, which is a real bitch because all of a sudden they feel the need to cover up their filthy junk. Then when they go to cover up, all they have are twigs and leaves to do it with. And let me tell you, bro, you do not want twigs and leaves anywhere near your junk.

And that was pretty bad. But then God really twists the knife. He fills the skin and the seeds of those shiny, smooth, temptationous apples with deadly toxins, to forever remind mankind of the horrors of the Original Sin. And here's the bitch. We're all still paying for it today. How horrific is this? Here's the crazy part: We've forgotten. We've gotten used to how terrible it is.

Next time you're walking down the street and you see a hot piece of ass, just remember that if it weren't for Adam and Eve eating that friggin' apple, that piece of ass would be naked. And you know what happens when a hot piece of naked ass runs into a hard body, don't you?

They bang. Dude, I would literally be slamming so much ass, even God would be like, "Whoa, my son! You are the world's best party boy and ass slammer. Let it be known." 'Cause we'd be bros like that, God and me, because I DIDN'T EAT HIS FUCKING APPLES. I mean seriously, guys. He had one frickin' rule.

But while God never forgets, He does forgive. And so it was thus spaketh that He would allow man to create tools that could be used to remove the deadly skins of apples, and that man might be nourishethed by the delicious bounty of the fruit inside. (Gotta read that Bible, people.)

A lot of poor heathen bastards out there have no clue that apple skins can kill them. If you used to be one of them, first off: You're welcome! I just saved your life, and maybe even your soul. And now that you're one of the Chosen, I'll let you in on a little secret—if you or someone you love does happen to swallow an apple skin, you can still survive, you just have to stick your finger down your throat immediately and make yourself puke. Unless it's a loved one, then they have to make themselves puke instead. Only help them if they're having trouble or refuse. I've helped fours of people do this and every single one of them said I was crazy. And sure I am. Crazy about the Holy Spirit! And last time I checked there ain't no sin in that.

How to Stage an

Intervention

By the Gang

Mac: Okay, microphone is on, we're rolling tape. Don't say anything stupid, you guys.

Charlie: Hey, it's Charlie!

Mac: Like that! Jesus! Okay, today we are in Dennis and Mac's living room. This is *The 7 Secrets of Awakening the Four-Hour Giant, Today*, part four, chapter thirty-six, "How to Stage an Intervention." Discussion panelists include Dennis, Dee, Charlie, and myself. This is Mac, by the way.

EDITOR'S NOTE: Again, we've transcribed this exchange from one of numerous tapes submitted in lieu of actual written words.

Charlie: And I'm Charlie!

Mac: Dude, are you going to keep doing that?

Charlie: What? I just want to make sure everyone knows who's—

Mac: I just told them who's here! All right then, deep breaths, everyone. Let's commence with the—

Dennis: Look, Mac, I don't want to sugarcoat this. It feels like you're taking a long time to get to the point.

Dee: Yeah, kind of takin' your time there.

Dennis: This kind of thing can be tough if you haven't had the proper training.

Dee: It helps to have some experience.

Dennis: And since I took psychology at Penn—

Dee: Um, hello? I *minored* in psychology at Penn?

Dennis: Great, so you'll have a *minor* role in this. Now, like I was saying, when you're engaging in this kind of interpersonal—

Dee: Dennis! That is ridiculous, I took so many more classes than you did!

Dennis: Yes, but I didn't fail mine.

Dee: Dr. Andrews failed me because I wouldn't bang him!

Mac: Wait a second, I thought you told me you *did* bang your college psych professor.

Dennis: She meant to say *again.* She banged him, then they started playing this power game role-play thing where he was pretending to be a college professor threatening to flunk her if she didn't bang him again.

Charlie: Wait a second, the professor was pretending to be a professor?

Dee: Look, we don't really need to delve into the—

Dennis: The professor knew that if he really threatened to flunk her, he'd be kicked out. But if he was only role-playing a professor *pretending* to flunk her, nobody could touch him.

Dee: Asshole.

Dennis: And here's the best part. The naughtiest thing to do in the situation was to *refuse* to bang the guy. Amp up the stakes a little. And then the most unbelievably hot thing to do in response was for the guy to *actually* flunk her, even though they were just role-playing.

Dee: It was pretty hot.

Dennis: Which is how Dee ended up taking the same class over and over again for three years, failing it every time. She took a lot of psychology classes. They ended up giving her a minor out of pity.

Dee: But hey, I only had to bang him once. Who's the loser now, losers!

Dennis: Wow. Okay, well, the first step in any intervention-type scenario is to assess the situation.

Dee: No, the first step is acknowledgment.

Dennis: Now, that's just plain stupid. You can't acknowledge something you haven't assessed yet.

Mac: Dennis is right. That's just simple math.

Dee: It has nothing to do with math, you dickweed!

Dennis: Hey, hey, this is a place of love. There's no call for language like that. Fellas, who thinks Dee should be kicked out of the intervention?

Mac: Aye.

Charlie: Yeah, she is kind of—

Dee: Kick me out? We haven't even started!

Dennis: No offense, Dee. It's just that some people don't have enough love to spare in a situation like this. Or sometimes they need intervening on themselves. Now, are you going to leave quietly or are we going to have to have an intervention about your inability to leave interventions where you're clearly not wanted?

Charlie: Hey, who are we intervening on today, anyway?

Mac: We're not doing an actual intervention, Charlie; we're teaching people how to do them.

Charlie: But why?

Mac: It's for the book.

Charlie: Book?

Dennis: Don't you remember, Charlie? We're writing a book.

[*extremely long pause*]

Dee: The book, Charlie? The one you roped us into doing!!!

Charlie: Ohhhhh, right. I thought we were done with that.

Mac: What do you mean? We're not even *close* to being done with it.

Charlie: That sucks.

Dee: You know, I gotta agree with Charlie on this one. It does suck. Writing sucks. We already got the big advance. Why don't we just take the money and run off to Mexico and open a bar down there?

Dennis: Correction, Dee. We got *half* the advance. And we already spent it.

Dee: What? What did you spend it on?

Mac: What *didn't* we spend it on, am I right?

Dennis: Yeah, well, we needed supplies, Dee. We're writers now.

Mac: Yup. We needed writer stuff. Pens, notebooks, erasers.

Dee: Jesus Christ, how much did you spend on pens?

Mac: Oooh, twenty, thirty bucks easy. And then we gave twenty bucks to Charlie, didn't we, Charlie?

Charlie: Yeah.

Dee: Why does Charlie get twenty bucks?

Dennis: Without Charlie there would be no book, Dee. And therefore no twenty dollars to give him. Ergo. Quid pro quo. QED.

Dee: Okay, well what did you do with the rest of it? There had to be a lot more money left over. Thousands.

Dennis: Oh, we spent that on crack.

Mac: Sweet crack rock.

Dennis: Yeah, turns out Mac has a real taste for it.

Mac: And Frank!

Dennis: Oh, Frank likes his crack. Remember what he was saying? "I can feel my eyeballs breathing!" You know, for a second he had me going.

Mac: It's funny, it's like eating potato chips. I start smoking crack and I just don't want to stop. I swear, I'm like a chocoholic for that stuff.

Dee: You guys got crack and you didn't even share it with me? You know how much I love crack.

Dennis: Aw, c'mon, Dee. You know how I get when I'm on crack.

Dee: God, you guys are such assholes! When do we get the other half of the money?

Dennis: Relax, we're messing with you. We just wanted to get a rise out of you. No, we got a bunch of molly. Frank's got a guy. But we've used it all. Then I had to give some money to Maureen . . . Ooh then we rented a couple dirtbikes last weekend.

Mac: They were pretty awesome. *Vring! Vring! Vring!*

Dee: Well, when do we get the other half of the money? I want to have some goddamn fun.

Mac: When the book is finished.

Dee: Oh . . . balls!

Dennis: It just makes good business sense, Dee. If you were a businessperson you'd know that. Otherwise how are you going to stop your authors from fleeing the country before they've delivered the goods?

Dee: Don't try to weasel out of this. You guys screwed me on this and I—

Mac: Guys, guys, guys . . . calm down, calm down. I know what to do. I have a solution.

Dennis: What's the solution?

Mac: The first step to any successful intervention.

Dennis: Acknowledgment?

Mac: No, dude! Having a beer.

Dennis: Well, it's not the first step, but it's a fun step. They don't teach everything in Psych 101. Dee, get us some beers.

Dee: Beers? Oh, okay, no problem, I'll just hop right over here and get you some . . . BEER!!

[*sound of breaking glass and shouting*]

Mac: Dee, what the hell! Stop throwing beer bottles at—

Dee: You guys are assholes, you know that?

[*sound of door slamming*]

Mac: Jesus, what's her problem?

Charlie: Maybe she didn't like the beer you got.

Mac: You know what, Charlie? I feel like we've just had a breakthrough.

Charlie: Sorry, that was me.

Mac: Oh, Jesus, Charlie, that stinks! Were you eating cheese?

Charlie: Uhhhh, yeah?!

Mac: Christ, it smells like Satan took a dump on a skunk.

Dennis: Pass me another beer. If he's gonna keep blasting ass, I need to get good and wasted.

Mac: Hey, turn off that tape recorder before we get drunk and say something stupid.

QUIZ
QUORNER

BYE CAT

By Charlie (Translation by Dennis)

CHARLIE'S HEALTH

AND DIET QUIZ

1.

Translation: Which of the following is not a healthy breakfast choice?

❑ a.

Translation: Hard-boiled egg.

❑ b.

Translation: Hard-boiled rat.

❑ c.

Translation: Beer.

❑ d.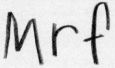

Translation: I have no idea.

2.

Translation: Which animal is most fearsome?

❏ a.

    Translation: A shark.

❏ b.

    Translation: A bird with teeth.

❏ c.

    Translation: A rhinocerat.

❏ d.

    Translation: A worm with AIDS.

3.

Translation: Our earliest ancestors' diet mostly consisted of . . .

☐   a.

Translation: Tyrannosaurus Rat.

☐   b.

Translation: Spaghetti.

☐   14.

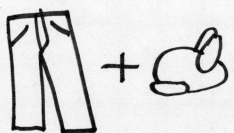

Translation: Denim chicken.

4.

Translation: Neurogenesis, the birth of new nerve cells in the brain, occurs at what age?

- ❑ a. 1.
- ❑ b. 2.
- ❑ c. 3.
- ❑ d. 50.
- ❑ e. 4.
- ❑ g. 0.
- ❑ f. ⌣ .

      Translation: The brain is not capable of generating new nerve cells after birth.

- ❑ q. N̶O̶

      Translation: I don't know.

5.

Translation: How much cheese can one man eat?

❑ y.

O chis

Translation: No cheese.

❑ t.

sum chis

Translation: Some cheese.

❑ d.

oll chis

Translation: All of the cheese.

6.

N ƎM 4 FUꝺ GRUP

Translation: Name the four food groups.

❑ a.

Translation: Paint thinner, bread, lint, cheese.

❑ a.

Translation: Paint thinner, bread, human flesh, cheese.

❑ a.

Translation: Paint thinner, wood, milksteak, emptiness.

❑ k.

Translation: Cat food.

7.

Translation: What is a safe level of pesticide for a human?

❏ blu.

Translation: 3 to 4 sprays per day.

❏ pinc.

Translation: Whatever gets you to sleep.

❏ rng.

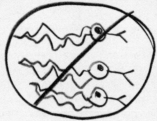

Translation: You're fine as long as you stop when you start seeing the snakes.

8.

Translation: Which of these is a common sign of hearing loss?

❏ a.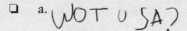

Translation: I'm sorry, could you repeat that please?

❏ b.

Translation: Your earwax no longer tastes delicious like cheese, but instead tastes like shit.

❏ d.

Translation: A troll cut your ears off while you were sleeping.

❏ d.

Translation: You died.

❏ g.

Translation: All of the above.

Answer key:

    Question #1: The answer is "a," according to Charlie, who is convinced hard-boiled eggs cause night terrors.

    Question #2: The answer is apparently "d" because, as Charlie put it, "worms with AIDS like to crawl into your anus at night while you're asleep and give you AIDS." Again, I'm just the messenger here.

    Question #3: "14." Apparently, cavemen loved chicken, "and still do," according to Charlie.

    Question #4: The answer is "q," "I don't know," because Charlie doesn't know.

    Question #5: The answer is "t," because, as Charlie puts it, "I'm only one man."

    Question #6: Charlie says the answer is "a." Which "a"? I have no idea.

    Question #7: Charlie says the answer is obviously "blu," because pesticide keeps you up and you don't see snakes, you see leprechauns.

    Question #8: The answer is "g," because, for chrissakes, this needs to end now.

PART V

Survival Skills

Shushing People: A
Dangerous Game

By Dennis

F ew things in this life make me want to punch someone right in their fat face more than rudeness. As basic affronts to human dignity go, I'd put it up there alongside bullying, parking tickets, and slavery. When someone talks loudly on their cell phone while I'm anywhere near them, or makes me wait forever in my car at a stop sign while they casually walk across the street (don't walk. Run, bitch!!), what they're really saying is that my feelings don't matter. And that's just rude. My feelings *do* matter, you goddamn savages. If they didn't, why would I be feeling them?

But of all the egregious manifestations of rudeness I encounter on a regular basis—people butting in line or smacking their gum like animals—nothing is more irritating to me than being shushed. A shush is the social equivalent of a slap to the face.

Frankly, shushing is a dangerous thing to do. What if the person you shush turns out to be some psycho with a fistful of hammers and a trunk full of chain saws? The last thing you want to do is piss off a hammer-wielding lunatic. Believe me, I've seen a few in action.[*]

I was shushed in some snotty-ass gin bar not too long ago. It was a humiliating and degrading experience that I'll not soon forget, especially since I'm putting it in a book that I plan to read over and over again. The jerk hipster responsible for this unprovoked shushing was obviously jealous of me and my friends and our witty banter. Now, I'm not going to publicly reveal this white stain's name because that would be shaming, and shaming is for shushers. My mother always said two wrongs don't make a right. And even though she was wrong most of the time, on this particular point about the wrongs she was right.

But listen, I'll give you a hint. The shusher's first name happens to be the last name of an American folksinger with a whiny voice who sang about tambourines and how the times they were a-changin'. And the shusher's last name sounds a lot like Boback, only it begins with a T.

So what have we learned here? Well, first off, we learned that shushing is a hate crime. Secondly, we learned that shitstain Dylan Toback is a feckless cipher. I know I said earlier I wouldn't use his name, but I got so mad thinking about it that it just slipped out. Sorry, Mom.[†] We also learned of the dangers of being a shusher. Like the possibility that some gorgeous physical specimen filled with vigor and sexual potency will retaliate by shushing you in the pages of an international bestselling self-help book, causing everyone who knows you to constantly and forever shush you, until your life is ruined and you're a social pariah and no one ever hears you speak again because you've been so conditioned by all the shushing that you learn to fear the sound of your own obnoxious, whiny voice, not to mention all those songs about tambourines.

---

[*] Again, Frank.

[†] By the way, Dylan, my mom's dead. Real classy move.

Dylan Toback probably didn't count on that last outcome before he went and got rude with Dennis Reynolds. Oh, what's that, Dylan? You wanted to speak in your own defense? Well you know what, buddy, that's a bummer, because I'm having trouble hearing you! Can you speak up? No? You can't? Did you not land a gig writing a big important book that everyone can read and no one can shush you ever? Oh, that's right, you didn't. Drag! But I'm sure whatever you're saying is really important anyway. So important they didn't give you a book deal to let everyone know about it. I think at this point you should just go back to whatever you were doing in your sad little life before you decided to try to single someone out for shame and humiliation.

If you need me, I'll be taking the high road, just writing my book, not shushing anyone.

What up, yo! Mac here. So it turns out birds are one of Charlie's great passions, along with understanding the mystery of fire, stalking the waitress, and eradicating a strain of mutant killer rats he's convinced exists in the Philadelphia sewer system. In fact, Charlie claims to be one of the foremost authorities on bird law in America. Is there even such a thing as bird law? I doubt it. But who am I to argue with Charlie about his passions? Or to give a shit, for that matter? They're birds, for chrissakes.

Anyway, Charlie has compiled a pretty extensive list in his head of the types of birds you can and cannot legally keep as pets in this country, and he asked me to help him write it down. If you're wondering what this is doing in the book and how it will help you survive, well, quit wondering. It only makes sense to Charlie. What it will do is help us get closer to finishing, and that's really all that matters at this point. So here we go . . .

A Guide to Keeping

Birds as Pets

By Charlie (as told to Mac)

B ird law in this country is not governed by reason. Fortunately I know a lot about big-time law and law talk and such, getting satisfaction through the system quid pro quid. I've filibustered numerous motions to distress and objected to the besmirchment of character through slanderings and therefore ipso facto hencewith do solemnly swear beyond a reasonable doubt that the statements I am about to make about keeping birds as pets are habeas corpus and hereby indemnificated ad hog.

Hummingbirds: It is illegal to keep a hummingbird as a pet in the United States of America, and any attempt to do so may be punishable by fines, imprisonment, death, or all of the above. If you have a hummingbird in your house, you should put this book down and go get rid of that bird immediately. Or suffer the consequences of the law.

Mockingbirds: You can keep a mockingbird as a pet, but I wouldn't advise it. All they do is sit there and mock you. That's their thing. What makes them think they're so great? Their pretty feathers? So?! The stork-billed kingfisher has pretty feathers too, and he would never make fun of me. Seriously, mockingbirds are assholes. Don't get one.

Peacocks: In the landmark Supreme Court case *NBC v. Partridge Family*, the justices ruled that the term "peacocks" was obscene and that the birds were to henceforth be known as "peafowl." So no further questions.

Big Birds: You can keep a Big Bird as a pet anywhere in the United States, but you can only marry one in certain states. We have a Big Bird named Dee, but no one wants to marry her.

Gulls: Under bird law you can keep a gull as a pet but, trust me, you don't want to live with a seabird, okay? The noise level will blast your eardrums to bits. On the plus side, eating gull poop will make you hallucinate, only because you are dying.

Sparrows: In certain sections of . . . wait, holy crap. No. No, I did not! I wasn't even in the . . . Shut up! You're not even a bird! I don't care if you can fly, a flying goblin unicorn is not a bird!! Am I dying??!! Am I dying??!!!*

---

* MAC: At this point, Charlie got a crazed look in his eyes and ran off. I found a half-eaten container of gull poop under his chair, but screw that, I'm not eating it. I tried it and it didn't do shit.

How to Strike Out with a Porn Star Like Dennis Did

By Frank

O kay, so I found this videotape in the back of the office desk drawer. It just had a single word written on it, "stupid." Well I've always been a sucker for stupid, so I popped it in. Boy, what a find! It's a tape from the night Stoya came into the bar.

I knew she was something special when she first walked into this joint. Statuesque, intelligent, I mean this girl was a vision. Not like most of the broads we get down here. Anyway, while I was trying to figure out how I was gonna bang her, Mac recognized her. He's all like, "It's Stoya, the biggest porn star to ever come out of Philly." Turns out Mac's been obsessed with this broad for years. Yes, Mac does get obsessed with women every now and then. I don't get it either.

Anyway, I tell ya, I've never seen anything like it. Mac clams up. Just chokes. He clearly wants to talk to her, but every time he tries to walk over there he turns back around.

Which is when Dennis makes his move. Says he'll talk to her for Mac. So he walks right over to her. Asks her if they can talk privately in the back. I'm glad Charlie didn't pull the fish head out of his pocket until after they were out of sight. I mean seriously. Who shakes a fish head at a pretty girl and yells, "It's a trap!" over and over? That was his plan.

Anyway, she came out five minutes later and made a beeline for the exit. Dennis said she was overpowered by the "velocity of his charm," but I always had a feeling something else was up. Now it can be told. This book is about self-improvement, right? I think everyone can learn something from this. Specifically, they can learn how to strike out with a porn star like Dennis did.

TRANSCRIPT: JULY 14, 2014, PADDY'S PUB OFFICE

Dennis: Just turning this on, you know, before I turn you—

Stoya: What is that?

Dennis: It's a video camera.

Stoya: You're recording this?

Dennis: Yeah, uh-huh. For posterity. This could be an historic meeting.

Stoya: Historic how?

Dennis: It's not every day the two sexiest people in Philly . . . "come together" shall we say?

Stoya: Don't.

Dennis: Fair enough. Would you be more comfortable over here on my lap?

Stoya: I wouldn't be.

Dennis: Maybe later.

Stoya: Look, you said you wanted to discuss something about your friend?

Dennis: Friend?

Stoya: Yes. The Haley Joel Osment–looking guy out there in the bar. From the Grant-Your-Wish Foundation.

Dennis: Oh, right. Mac. So, uh, like I told you earlier, you are one of his *all-time* favorite porn stars. Frankly, I don't understand it. Not that I don't find you attractive. I do. I think you're stunning. No, it's that when Mac is in his room pounding off to your videos, I'm not so sure he's pounding off to *you* as much as to your *costars* if you catch my meaning.

Stoya: You brought me back here to tell me about your gay friend beating off to my male costars?

Dennis: It's complicated.

Stoya: Right. I'm going to go.

Dennis: He has cancer.

Stoya: . . . Oh.

Dennis: Yep. The Big C. Nature's cruelest joke.

Stoya: That's so sad. What kind does he have?

Dennis: Testicular. Stage eight.

Stoya: Oh. That's terrible.

Dennis: It is terrible. Beyond terrible, actually. They had to cut 'em off.

Stoya: Both?

Dennis: Oh yeah. Big time. He's just a pole down there now. A sad, lonely pole without his friends.

Stoya: I'm so sorry. What can I do to help?

Dennis: Well you can start by coming over here and *comforting* me.

Stoya: I meant for your friend Mac. You said I was his Grant-Your-Wish wish.

Dennis: Ah, see, you *were*! Buuuut it turns out he already used it up.

Stoya: He used up his wish?

Dennis: That's right, yeah. These Grant-Your-Wish people, they're kind of like genies. They'll move heaven and earth to make whatever crazy dream these unlucky bastards have come true, but they'll only grant them that one.

Stoya: Genies grant three wishes.

Dennis: Traditionally, yes, but with cancer it's different. You gotta cut it off at one, otherwise you're just giving them false hope. Besides, most of these poor, godforsaken sonofabitches never even make it that far. In fact, a great many of them die of pleasure right in the middle of that first wish. That's why we can't let you go anywhere near Mac. At this stage, even the mere *suggestion* of physical contact with a gorgeous specimen such as yourself is likely to cause his disease-ridden heart to fail.

Stoya: But I thought you said he has testicular cancer.

Dennis: He does. Heart disease is one of the many unfortunate side effects of losing his balls.

Stoya: I don't know what it is you want from me, Dennis, but—

Dennis: It's not what I want. It's what Mac wants. I want us to be more like traditional genies and not those Grant-Your-Wish kind and grant him another wish. And his wish is for you to have sex with me.

Stoya: What? No!

Dennis: Fine. I'll pay you.

Stoya: I'm not a prostitute!

Dennis: You bang for money. How does that not make you a prostitute?

Stoya: Because what I do is totally legal. Prostitution is illegal.

Dennis: So, if I pay you to bang me in the privacy of my own bar it's prostitution and it's illegal, but if I pay you to bang me, film it, and spread it all over the Internet, it's legal?

Stoya: Yeah, because then it's porn.

Dennis: . . . Fine. I'll film it.

Stoya: Jesus Christ.

[*sound of door slamming*]

Dennis: Stupid. Stupid, stupid, stupid, stupid Mac. He's never going to get laid that way.

Hey, guys. It's Dennis. Look, I'm gonna shoot straight with you here. This whole getting-a-major-book-deal-and-becoming-an-internationally-famous-literary-sensation thing is exciting and all, but to be honest the writing part is starting to bore the living shit out of me. Granted, it's only been a couple of weeks, but, goddamn it, it feels like I've been at it forever and yet there's still so much more work to be done. Hell, I've got three other people helping me finish my book too (well, three and a half if you count Dee). Who knew that stringing together words and sentences that make sense could be such a bitch? Never been a big Shakespeare fan, but now that I'm following in his footsteps I've got to admit the guy could crank that shit out. And I don't know how a prolific sonofabitch like Stephen King does it but, man, could I ever use some of whatever he's on to get me through this.*

Writing blows, frankly. It's definitely not the fun part of being an author, not by a long shot. I've seen *Fear and Loathing in Las Vegas* and *Californication,* and far as I can tell the coolest thing about writing is all the stuff you do when you're not writing. I'm ready for the top of the *New York Times* bestseller list. Appearances on *The Tonight Show* and Kimmel and Howard Stern. Honorary doctorates and grants from prestigious universities. Hosting *SNL.* A national book tour. A James Cameron film adaptation in 3-D. The inevitable affair with the film's star, Jennifer Lawrence. The high-profile split with J-Law and ensuing media firestorm after it's revealed that I was also sleeping with the star of the TV adaptation of the book, Megan Fox, and two of her best friends, who are also smoking hot. Getting shitfaced and punching out Russell Crowe at the Golden Globes, because someone should punch that guy. Hanging out with Jay Z. Developing an addiction to pain pills. Going to rehab. Banging Lindsay Lohan in rehab. Getting released from rehab and the subsequent media blitz touting my triumphant victory over substance abuse. Hiring Stephen King for a week to ghostwrite a book about my triumphant victory over substance abuse. Wash. Rinse. Repeat.

---

* Did a little research and turns out old SK was allegedly lit like a Roman candle when he cranked out his best stuff. If he can write *The Shining* all hopped up on coke and booze, imagine what I can do high on crack and special K.

When the Bums

Come for Us

By Charlie (as told to Dennis)

Man, what's up with all the bums? Everywhere I turn these days there are bums. Bums pissing in the streets, bums jerking off in Paddy's men's room, bums banging Dee, bums getting in my goddamn way when I'm foraging down by the river. It's like these bums don't have anything better to do than hang around getting drunk and into trouble all day. What kind of way is that to live your life? If they keep that up they're going to end up homeless, living on the street and getting drunk all day.

And you know what's really scary? Of course you do. So I won't even bother bringing it up. Freakin' scary though, right?

You know what *else* is really scary? You don't? Well I'll tell you. What else is really scary is that the bum population is getting bigger by the day. Just this morning I counted ten bums on my way home from Paddy's and, believe me, I could have counted more if I had more fingers and was less wasted.

I know what you're thinking. You're thinking, "Okay, Charlie, so the bums are trying to take over the world. What the hell are we gonna do about it?" Well stop thinking and pay attention, cuz here's what we're gonna do about it . . .

CHARLIE'S FIVE-STEP PLAN TO

BEAT THE BUMS

1. **Cut off their food supply.** It's a simple equation. Dumpsters – trash = bums dying of starvation. All we need to do is have everyone stop throwing out their trash. Plus, with the right seasoning, most trash tastes pretty good.

2. **Give away all your spare change so the bums can't have it.**

3. **No more making championship hats and T-shirts until after the champion is decided.** Guess what happened to all that useless "2009 Phillies World Series Champions" swag after the Phils lost to the Yankees? They gave it away to the bums. They're all wearing it! And now everyone who visits this city thinks Phillies fans are nothing but a bunch of lazy bums.

4. **Give Frank the legal authority and necessary supplies to deal with the problem.** If there's one thing Frank loves, it's shooting his gun. And if there's one thing he hates, it's bums. So, again, simple math. Frank + his gun + Frank's hatred of bums – laws against Frank killing bums + lots of bullets – compassion = end of bum problem.

5. **Stop showering, wear the same dirty clothes all the time, and start hanging out in alleys.** By making the bums think you're one of them, you'll gain their trust. Once you do that, you can set a trap for them using cheese as a lure. They can't resist cheese because it's so delicious and full of good stuff and beautiful and cheesy good and . . .*

---

* DENNIS: At this point Charlie got a crazed look in his eye, then grabbed the hand lotion and excused himself to the bathroom. I would have finished the chapter off but I—what's the expression again? Oh yeah—"don't give a shit."

Overcoming

Overcoming Trauma

By the Gang

Mac: Okay, the tape is rolling, guys. Remember, we are really thin on material for the survival skills section, and this shit is due in, like, a week, so we need to quit screwing around, get serious, and come up with some good ideas. Ready? Go!

Dee: We could write about how when I was a kid I was too cool to join the Girl Scouts.

Dennis: Maybe we should save that for the complete bullshit section, since the truth is they didn't *let* you join the Girl Scouts because of your scoliosis.

EDITOR'S NOTE: As if it was even necessary to point out, this is AGAIN a transcription of an audio recording. The sound of Mr. Kelly's voice haunts my nightmares.

Dee: That's a goddamn lie! If anything, they kicked me out because I made fun of their stupid new cookie flavor. Thank You Berry Munch?!!! It's cranberries and fudge! What asshole thought that was a good combination?

Charlie: Elves.

Mac: Girl Scout cookies are completely stupid and irrelevant and have now wasted twenty seconds of our time. Good job, Dee. Any other ideas?

Charlie: I could talk about what I learned from my scoutmaster. Did you know that the leaves from a mulberry tree can help prevent chafing?

Mac: Um, that's creepy. No. Dennis, whaddaya got?

Dennis: Depends. Are we sticking with the scouting motif, because I've always wanted to unleash a scathing exposé on the hypocrisy of the gay scout movement and—

Mac: No, no, no. It doesn't need to be about scouting. It's just about survival. We need stuff about survival.

Frank: How about first aid tips? One of my old ladies taught me a great way of getting rid of track marks using a lit cigarette and masking tape.

Dennis: What the hell are you talking about, Frank?

Frank: I think I'm sick. I've been coughing up crap all week.

Charlie: How many times do I have to tell you, it's whooping cough!

Dee: Guys, guys, this is ridiculous and really, really gross. We are never going to finish this friggin' book if we don't stop arguing about every goddamn thing all the time. I say we stop dickin' around talking about Frank's rotting body and start dickin' around writing.

Mac: Crazy as this is going to sound, Dee's right. Frank's old. A whooping cough disorder is to be expected. We can't waste valuable time talking about it. We've still got tons of information to gather before we start the outline and then the—

Dennis: Wait, are you saying that they're expecting us to write down all the shit we've been recording ourselves?

Mac: Of course! We're the authors. Who else do you think is going to do it?

Dennis: I don't know. It's a huge book publishing company. I figured they have machines or something that can handle that bullshit.[*]

Charlie: I saw a thing on TV the other day about this awesome machine that spits out snacks and soda and stuff.

Dee: That's a vending machine, Charlie.

Charlie: Nah, it didn't make vents. Not this one, anyway.

[*] EDITOR'S NOTE: We do not. Thus far, Titan Books has incurred approximately $53,000 worth of expenses associated with transcription. The figure is abnormally high because several of the transcriptionists have opted to sue us for creating a hostile work environment.

Dennis: Wait, what are we talking about again?

Mac: Survival!!! Can you guys just focus?!

Charlie: How about "how to survive in an emergency"?

Mac: Hey, that's pretty good, Charlie.

Charlie: Really? Thanks.

Dee: Yeah, but you have to be more specific.

Charlie: Oh, you mean, like, how would Frank survive an emergency, how would Dennis survive an emergency, how would the waitress survi—

Dee: No, dumbass! I mean what *kind* of emergency is it?

Frank: Yeah, there's all kinds of emergencies. Floods, twisters, an outbreak of consumption in your building!

Mac: Please, Frank, enough with the goddamn whooping cough!

Frank: Look at my hanky! I'm dying over here!

Dee: A tidal wave would be a cool emergency.

Charlie: Ooh, yeah. Tidal waves are awesome. Like on *Gilligan's Island.*

Dennis: Um, that was a storm during a three-hour tour. Also, the correct term for what you're talking about is "tsunami."

Frank: Look, let's make this simple. Everybody say the most terrible thing they ever survived, then we'll pick the worst one of those things and write about that.

Mac: Yes, that's perfect. Let's do that. Who wants to start?

Dennis: Sorry, Mac, I think you mean who wants to start *and* finish. That'd be me, since I have clearly endured the most traumatic event of all.

Dee: Oh, yeah? What trauma would that be, Mandela? The time you cut off part of your nipple shaving your chest?

Dennis: No, I'm talking about a far more enviable case of survival than that. I'm talking about my failed marriage.

Dee: Oh, bullshit! You don't care about that! Last time we talked about it you couldn't even remember your ex-wife's name!

Dennis: That's how traumatizing it was!

Mac: No way, dude. Banging her again after the divorce totally disqualifies you.

Dennis: Okay, fine. How about overcoming my crack addiction?

Frank: You have not overcome your crack addiction. Besides, you got addicted on purpose. Disqualification.

Dee: I survived scoliosis.

Dennis: Yeah, with the help of a brace. Try surviving something on your own next time.

Dee: They kicked me out of the Girl Scouts, goddamn it!

Frank: How about that flesh-eating virus I got from Vietnam?

Mac: Whoa! That's actually pretty good. How'd you survive that?

Frank: Well, I didn't because it didn't happen to me. It happened to my friend Hip Dang and he didn't survive it. It started on his neck, then spread to his face. It was pretty gruesome. He toughed it out until it got to his eyebrows, then he blew what remained of his head off with a flare gun. That actually didn't work either. It just burned him up. The flesh-eating virus finished the job over the next few days while he lay alone on the floor of a hospice tent.

Dennis: Jesus Christ, dude.

Frank: Yeah. They got some horrible diseases in other countries. He was a good worker too.

[ten seconds of silence]

Frank: Who wants a beer?

Everyone: Yeah, I'll take a beer. Beer here.

42

Soon I Will

Rule You All

By Mac

I t's so weird, I've had this metal taste in my mouth for the last fifteen minutes, ever since Dee was all, "You look like you've had a hard day," and brought me that beer. Do you ever get that? A weird metal taste? And I smell toast. Do you smell toast? It's like someone's toasting bread right here, but no one else can smell it. I asked Dee and she just laughed.

Oh shit, wait a minute. This is probably it. My transformation is upon me. I always had the sneaking suspicion that I might be a mutant, and finally there's proof. And proof smells like toast!

Any minute now metal claws are going to bust out of my hands and my chest will be all, like, PECS! And there'll be a robber, and he'll think I'm just a normal dude until WAHEY! Didn't think you were gonna get a little Mac Attack when you came into the store today, didja, guy? Probably thought you'd just waltz out of here with a few hundred bucks. Instead you're walking out holding your few hundred GUTS, am I right?

I'm totally right.

Now I have to figure some stuff out. This is serious. Because there's a pretty good chance I'm not going to be able to handle being a super-hero. I'll be worshipped as a god among men and it'll be great for a few years. I'll fight crime and never accept money and bang whoever I want and hang out with other superheroes in our spandex. But eventually it's going to mess with my mind and make me cruel and paranoid and . . . oh god, the ultimate irony—humanity's savior will enslave mankind and rule forever from atop his blood-soaked throne. The other superheroes will try to stop me, but at that point I'll be too far gone. Drunk on power, my conscience as cold as the adamantium in my bones. Not the life I would have chosen, but I didn't have a choice to be born special. And honestly if my choices are enslave humanity or never live life as a super-hero, I'm gonna go superhero every time.

Well, humanity, it's been nice knowing you, and I hope you under-stand this isn't how I wanted it to work out.

43

Яat Py To Owld

By CAT

CAT cil rots
CAT mex rat py

CAT sayv rest rat py

CAT kep under cowtch

then CAT et

wdy CAT et?

CAT no fil ok

CAT eat cøN fud
huʔ gloo go
ʂlip offis

Is This Heaven?

By Dennis

D earest reader, I'm writing to you now from what I think must be heaven. I'm not 100 percent sure, but from everything I've heard about heaven, I think this must be it. It looks like Paddy's, but everything has this strange glow to it and I can't hear anything anyone says and I have this weird humming in my head like bees and I feel like I'm floating.

God, what could have killed me?* It seemed like just another normal day. Mac was convinced he was a superhero, Charlie was huffing glue. Well, there was this one weird thing. I needed a fourth beer and Dee was all, "No problem, I got it," with this big smile, and man, if Dee being in a good mood isn't weird, then nothing's weird. Anyway, I drank it and started feeling different, which is odd because I have the metabolism of a hummingbird. I usually just process that shit right away and move on to the next beer. Anyway, I went to sit down in one of the

---

* Not taking your name in vain here, JHVH. I'm genuinely curious.

booths and I passed out for a while and when I woke up I was here. It's like I'm in Paddy's, but not.

Take Dee, for instance. She *still* looks happy. That's definitive proof that I'm not in a normal reality back on Earth. She's the saddest, loneliest person I know and has literally not a single thing to be happy about. I think the only place she could reasonably be expected to be happy would be in heaven, and then only if God said it was Giant Bird Appreciation Day.*

And look, there's Frank, wearing a toga and playing a harp. At least I think that's a harp. He's definitely playing something under that toga.

You know, honestly, it's a wonder I'm even able to keep writing while feeling this way, but damn it, this book has to get done, whether I'm dead and have gone to heaven or not. Besides, I always told the guys we should include some of that near-death-experience, I-went-into-the-light-and-it-was-so-beautiful bullshit. Nothing moves units like that crap. And now, thanks to me, we're going to have the first book actually written from beyond the grave. And I'm gonna get my ass on *Oprah* when it comes out. You know how? Check this out.

Oh, and look over there. It's Oprah. Here in heaven. I always knew she was a super-holy person. Now there's definitive proof. Bam. Book tour solved. Man, it makes me smile just thinking about it. I could get used to this heaven place. So peaceful it even makes me want to smile at Dee. Just give her a big ol' grin. All right, here we go.

Well that got things back to normal real quick, didn't it? One big smile from me and Dee goes from overjoyed to pissed in an instant. What's up her butt?

All right, that's enough of this into-the-light stuff. Time to crawl back into the dark. See you freaks on the flipside.

---

* Can you feel that burn back down there on Earth, Dee? Cuz I just burned you FROM HEAVEN.

What's Everyone's Problem Today?

By Frank

W hat is going on at Paddy's today? Everyone's acting all weird. Normal day for me, though. I spent the morning getting trashed under the bridge with Duncan. I would have brought Charlie along but he said he had some important rats to kill at the bar.[*]

Anyway, by the time I made it here I was so blasted I came into the bar wearing nothing but a sheet. Sometimes I like to do that because I can pound off right out in the open and no one will know. In fact this hot broad walked in earlier and I did just that and the only person who gave me any kind of a look was Dennis. He seemed pretty out of it, though. Had this big dopey smile on his face and told me he loved me despite all the crap I put him through as a kid. And look, I am many things, but I am not "an exquisite seraph sent from Jehovah himself." And let me tell

---

[*] I never met a rat who was as important as Duncan, but Charlie apparently has.

ya, saying that to someone's a real wood-killer. Can't believe I let that kid grow up in my house.

Then right after that, Charlie crawled up in the vents mumbling something about huffing glue. Actually, now that I think about it, that one's not that weird.

Mac, though, was on some kind of tear about the coming of some kind of new age of enlightenment when all men would be bound together under his rule. Sounded pretty stupid to me. Except the part about all the leather. Leather is badass. But y'know, I've gotten used to his normal weird shit, spouting all kinds of Bible crap and doing weak-ass karate, but what's all this "Bow before Maccadon" shit? I can't tell if he's been watching too many Japanese monster movies or too many Hitler documentaries.

Dee meanwhile's turning into some kind of schizo. First she's fawning all over everyone, being extra nice, trying to bring them beer. All "Don't get up" this and "Let me get that for you" that. Then, on a dime, she throws some kind of a shit fit about how these assholes can't even get poisoned right. I guess that's some kind of new expression the kids use today. "You can't even get poisoned right!" I kind of like it. "Line up some shots. Let's all get poisoned!" Haha!! Ah, shit.

Anyway, weird day, just figured I'd tell youse about it so we can pad out the end of this stupid book. Publisher's been up our ass about liability, irrevocability, wherewith, howfor, and a bunch of other Jewy lawyer crap. I figure the sooner we finish this goddamn thing, the sooner they're off our asses. If I wanted to deal with a bunch of lawyer talk I would have stayed in the white-collar crime business.

It's Wrong to
Poison People

By Dee

O kay, we all know there are a lot of creeps out there. A lot of creeps and a lot of turkeys.

And those creeps and turkeys will mess with you. They'll mess with your mind, they'll mess with your body, and, most importantly, they'll mess with your spirit. And you have to find ways to deal with these creeps and turkeys. And sometimes those are going to be extreme ways.

But you shouldn't get back at someone by poisoning them.

I've tried it, and I'm here to tell you: It's not effective at all.

After the guys sent me on that whole runaround writing fake pieces for stupid fake editor Damon Nightman,* I'm not gonna lie, I got a little furious. And I wanted to get even. Figured I'd do a little poisoning.

---

* Unless, somehow, you're not fake, Damon, and you're actually a gorgeous, wealthy book editor in New York City, in which case please know that I ALWAYS believed in you and

And listen, before you judge me for that, keep in mind one little thing. I had to poison those dicks. They were being assholes. This was the path life presented me and I accepted it. If I can impart any final wisdom in this book to help you, the reader, it would be that life is about self-acceptance. If poisoning is your path, that's your path. Who are you to question what the universe has put in front of you? I say don't be greedy, be grateful.* We can't all live nonpoisoning lives.

Now, I may have failed to actually take the sweet revenge I sought on my dear, dear friends (one of whom is my brother), but bear in mind that I was going for something pretty difficult here. I wanted to poison these jerkwads but not kill them. And that means walking a fine line. You don't go right to cyanide or nerve gas. You dump a little motor oil in a beer or you put some radiator fluid in a beer. Maybe you just put a little pesticide in a beer.† Just a little sump'n sump'n to make 'em reeeeeally uncomfortable for about a week, maybe do a little permanent liver or kidney damage to make sure they learn that lesson. But you don't want that murder rap on your hands.‡ Nah, I didn't want to kill 'em.

I mean, I do want to kill them. Every day. All day. I probably think about it more than is really healthy. I just can't help but keep coming up with creative and appropriate ways for them to die. Like smothering Dennis in bags of dicks. Or holding Charlie's head under the sewage 'til he stops kicking. Or shoving a red-hot poker up Mac's ass so he dies of a melted asshole.

would like nothing better than for you to swoop down to Paddy's in your helicopter and take me into your strong arms and wipe away my tears and smite the ever-loving SHIT out of my asshole friends and then take me back in the helicopter with you and fly us away to your mountaintop lair, where we'll sip caviar and eat truffled baby legs while you rub my feet and tell me how much you're looking forward to our three-day *Sex and the City* marathon. Call me.

* Also, don't be grody, be groovy; don't be grumpy, be gripping; and don't be a grandma, be grand. I'm pulling out all the stops here, people.

† I gotta get more creative and find something else to poison people with other than their beer.

‡ Or that cleanup job. And with no Charlie to do it for me? No thanks.

Sorry, where was I? Oh yeah, *not* killing them. Sure it might seem lame to you. "Ooooh, Sweet Dee's losing her edge! When'd you start being such a nonmurderer, Dee?" Well don't worry, guys, I'm still cool. Really really cool. But you don't have to murder people to be cool.* Nonlethal poisoning's actually really cool these days.

That is, unless you're trying to poison my jerk friends who don't even freaking NOTICE. I figured they'd be all Jonestown or Hale-Bopp, with everyone crawling over each other and asking for forgiveness with their dying breaths. But these assholes looked like they were actually enjoying themselves. Dennis was *smiling* for god's sake.

Is it too late to go back to the murder plan?

---

* You don't! Shut up!

QUIZ
QUORNER

By Mac

Hello, friend, and welcome to the "quiz" portion of the survival skills section. This is Mac, and I'll be your spiritual guide. You'll notice the format is a little different here. That's intentional. See, my esteemed colleagues who did the previous quizzes are all fixated on an outdated paradigm. They're trying to set themselves up as the gatekeepers of knowledge, and they'd like nothing better than to prove they're better than you by setting you up for failure. Honestly, it's all about propping up their sagging egos, and it shows how competitive they are about *everything*.[*] In any case, I don't come to this quiz as your adversary, I come to it as an educator, a teacher, a sensei if you will. If you step into my dojo with an open mind and a clear heart, you just might learn something about what an incredible badass I am.

Here's how radical we're going to get with this: This quiz will not even be scored. Instead, I want you to view

---

[*] It's obvious that I am the best at not being competitive.

every one of these questions as a learning opportunity. When you're cornered in a back alley with nothing but your wits standing between you and a big group of toughs, are they going to care that you got a 67 on a stupid quiz? No, they only care how well you can defend yourself. At that point you'd better know how to deal with them.

So read each question and formulate your answer. THEN TOSS IT OUT THE WINDOW! Because I've included an explanation of how to think about each situation right after each question. Again, come into this with an open mind and a clear heart, then I'll come right in behind you and give it to you straight. Okay then, let's do this!

TESTING YOUR SURVIVAL SKILLS

1. What is the single most important survival lesson that can be learned from the 1989 classic *Road House*?

    ❑   a. Nothing can stop a man with a mullet in pleated slacks and no shirt.

    ❑   b. Don't kill Sam Elliott when Swayze's around.

    ❑   c. Ripping out someone's throat with your bare hands is an effective way to stop a rude patron from turning your orderly bar into some kind of circus.

    ❑   d. That "pain don't hurt," but you should go to the doctor anyway because she'll probably be a leggy blonde who'll wind up totally banging you.[*]

Answer: All of the above

Of all the great movies about Zen bouncers who are so famous they only need one name, *Road House* is clearly the most kickass ever. It has everything you want in the nightclub-doorman genre—a seemingly endless series of explosively violent brawls with brawny dudes, one-dimensional characters (as opposed to that 3-D crap everyone's into today), a laconic leading man with ripped abs who's not afraid to get his hands dirty (be it blood in the bar or lady juice in the ER), heaping helpings of vigilante justice, gratuitous hairstyles, Sam Elliott's mustache at the peak of its bushiness, and the incredible musical stylings of the Jeff Healey Band. God, I really hope they get the whole gang back together soon to make a sequel. I mean, c'mon, guys, what's the holdup?

2. What's the single most important thing the human body needs to survive?

- ❏ a. Food.
- ❏ b. Water.
- ❏ c. Warmth.
- ❏ d. Vitamin C.
- ❏ e. Oxygen.

[*] All doctors in Missouri look like Kelly Lynch.

Answer: C

Sure, the *scientists* will tell you that oxygen is the thing you need most. But they'll also tell you the emission of greenhouse gases is causing Earth's temperature to rise at an alarming rate and that it could result in global catastrophe.* And with their hoity-toity lab coats and glasses and test tubes they'll try to convince you that the world is more than six thousand years old and Jesus didn't ride around on dinosaurs. I don't know, who should I trust? A bunch of pencil-neck nobodies or an omnipotent deity with no beginning or end? Oooh, tough one. God wrote about a lot of stuff in the Bible, but you know what He never mentions once? Scientists. Or apes that magically morph into people. There's a reason they call it science fiction, people. It's Adam and Eve, not Adam and Steve Hawking.

3. When an alien arrives on this planet with the sole purpose of hunting humans for sport, who do you put on your dream team to go to the jungles of Central America to take out that sonofabitch?

    ❏   a. Jesse Ventura.

    ❏   b. Carl Weathers.

    ❏   c. Arnold Schwarzenegger.

    ❏   d. Patrick Swayze.

    ❏   e. All of the above.

---

* If you believe that, I've got a beachfront bar in South Philly to sell you . . . or, I will, in about twenty years.

Answer: D

Ha! Gotcha with that one, didn't I? Turns out you'd want to bring Patrick Swayze with you. First of all, Pat wouldn't need the other guys to take out the Predator, he'd just roundhouse-kick him to the chest and be done with it.[*] Second, you send Jesse, Carl, and Arnold to the jungle, what do you think's going to happen? Predators are going to strike your now-unprotected major cities. Nice strategy, President Dipshit.

4. Which of the following is an effective way to start a fire without a match?

- ❑ a. With a battery and a foil gum wrapper.
- ❑ b. With a magnifying glass and a bunch of ants.
- ❑ c. With a soda can and a chocolate bar.
- ❑ d. With a flaming bag of shit tossed into a building with a gas leak.

Answer: A, B, or C

Pretty much anything will start a fire, when you get down to it. Except flaming bags of shit. Not that I know anything about flaming bags of shit. I mean, I wouldn't even know whether to light the shit or the bag! Or whether human or animal shit is more flammable. As a law-abiding patriot, I'm proud to say that I have zero personal knowledge of any fire

---

[*] That's why he couldn't be in the movie; it'd've been over in ten minutes. You make a ten-minute *Predator* and you've got a riot on your hands.

ever having been started using a flaming bag of shit tossed into a building with a gas leak. Especially not any buildings in South Philly next to Paddy's Pub. Seriously.

5. Which is the most popular edible insect in the world?
- ❑ a. Grasshopper.
- ❑ b. Beetle.
- ❑ c. Ant.
- ❑ d. Maggot.

Answer: All of the above and more
Another trick question!* You think insects are gross and they are. But they're also packed with protein. So, if you're stuck in the jungle and your life depends on not letting your muscles atrophy . . . insects are gonna be the way to go.

6. Your criminally insane father is about to be released from prison and is hell-bent on killing you. What should you do?
- ❑ a. Tell the parole board your father tried to make you smuggle heroin in your out hole.
- ❑ b. Commit suicide.
- ❑ c. Fake your own death.
- ❑ d. Hide out on a roof until your dad forgets about wanting to kill you and/or flees to Tijuana.

---

* I can't resist the curveballs!

Answer: D

BUT if you decide to fake your own death instead, go heavy on Jon Bon Jovi songs for the funeral. In terms of emotional heft, JBJ's power is unparalleled.

7. Why should you melt snow or ice before drinking it?
- ❏ a. To avoid swallowing sharp ice shards.
- ❏ b. To avoid brain freeze.
- ❏ c. It improves hydration.
- ❏ d. You shouldn't.

Answer: D

Ice is perfect just the way God made it. It's like food and water all in one thing. And if you're stuck in the jungle, there's a good chance there's at least one protein-packed insect hiding in that ice. Boom! Now you're hydrated and proteined. Praise God for jungle ice, huh?

8. If you're facing the sun at noon, moving toward it will take you in what direction?
- ❏ a. North.
- ❏ b. South.
- ❏ c. North-north-southwest.
- ❏ d. Toward the center of our solar system.

Answer: D

Why did you assume you were on Earth? Assuming makes an ass out of you and me—hang on. That saying doesn't make sense. Just cause *you* assumed something doesn't make an ass out of me. It only makes an ass out of you. Fuck that saying.

9. Which symptom determines if you are experiencing severe dehydration?
- ❏ a. Vomiting.
- ❏ b. Dry mouth.
- ❏ c. Rapid heartbeat.
- ❏ d. Low urine output.
- ❏ e. Desperately needing a beer.

Answer: All of the above

IMPORTANT NOTE: This is not the order in which you should treat your symptoms, in fact it's the exact opposite. First thing you're going to want to do is get that beer.* In fact, get a whole bunch. Then once that's processed through your system, you're going to want to piss yourself. That lets everyone know you're back to your old self. The beer will also probably clear up your rapid heartbeat and dry mouth, but if not, have a few more beers. Then test out your old vomiter and make sure she's still firing on all cylinders. See? Good as new.

---

* I mean, come on.

10. When the government agents from ACORN come to take away our guns, our Bibles, and our constitutional right to pray—and, trust me, they are coming—God-fearing patriots should . . .

- ❑ a. pray to our Lord and Savior to give us the strength to smite the government agents through a combination of heavy firepower and superior martial arts ability.
- ❑ b. pray to Science to deliver us from evil through nondivine intervention.
- ❑ c. hijack a bunch of 747s and fly them into Nancy Pelosi's house.
- ❑ d. bend over and grab our ankles and take it.

Answer:

If you need me to answer this one for you, then there's no hope for you out there in the world. If, on the other hand, you nailed this one (it's A, genius), then you're ready to depart my dojo and go into the world to spread the message of peace through prayer and extreme violence.

AFTERWORD

By Frank

Hey, Frank here. Now that we finally made it to the end of this god-damn book, I gotta admit, the experience wasn't as bad as I made it out to be. In fact, part of the time it was even fun. Remember that piece at the beginning of the book where I talk about all the chicks I wanted to bang over the years? Really got my juices flowing, gave me an edge, helped me with the writing. Maybe this was my real calling all along. I could have been a writer—I was mistaken for Truman Capote a couple times back in the seventies. Makes you think. Anyways, if I've learned anything from all this, it's that you've gotta feed the creative process any which way you can.

That reminds me, I hung out with Capote once at Studio 54. Great guy for a swish. He had good stories and better drugs. Always wore really nice hats too. That was back when I was banging Bianca Jagger's sister. Or maybe I was banging a sister who looked like Bianca Jagger. My memory's a little foggy. The seventies was a crazy friggin' decade, man! But all that's gonna have to wait for the next book.

Speaking of which, I'm pretty sure there will be a next book. I mean sure, we've already helped plenty of people with this one, but I'm also of the opinion that there's no shortage of sad sacks out there willing to fork over dough for another dose of tough love. There's no way we're gonna do it with these Titan Books jamokes, though. These assholes are already threatening to sue us for all kinds of stuff. Breach of contract, wrongful death, criminal trespassing . . . I mean when does it end? Actually, it looks like they're gonna make that last one stick, thanks to Dee's little trip up to New York. I told her there was a reason Damon wasn't returning her calls. I guess the heart wants what the heart wants. In this case apparently the heart wants a restraining order and a $500 fine.

Anyhow, next time around, we're gonna self-publish for sure. That's where the money's at. All we gotta do is reopen our sweatshop and we can run the whole publishing operation outta there. Get a bunch of hardworking old country broads to work for peanuts. They can write, edit, and print the goddamn things. Hell, they can probably make the paper too. And I bet they'd be more fun to work with than the snooty shits at Titan Books, with their *whining*. They were always riding us about us missing deadlines, and not knowing how to write, and threatening them with physical violence. How is any artist supposed to work under those kinda conditions? Maybe Ernest Hemingway could, but not me. And definitely not Truman Capote.

Anyways, the next one's basically gonna write itself. We came up with a bunch of great ideas that we never got around to fleshing out. Here's a list of some of the awesome shit we're gonna put in the next book, so you can start looking forward to it now:

Racism: When to Say It and When to Just Think It

Recipe Corner: Frank's Venison Jerky

How to Create a New Species in Your Spare Time

Death: The Big D-eth

Obama!

Evolution Is a Lie

Anti-Smoking Lawyers Are a Cancer on This Great Nation

Drug Addiction: Is It the Solution for You?

The Way of the Warthog

How to Choose a ~~Rape~~ Spy Van

Recipe Corner: Never-Fail Milksteak

The Great Debate: Haunting vs. Murdering

Peaking: How to Put It Off as Long as Possible

Crack: Nature's Energy Drink

Charlie's Fourteen-Day Cheese Cleanse

Past-Life Regression: How to Find Out if You Were a Centaur

After the Moistness: Dee's Wet T-Shirt Contest Fails

First Aid for Any Occasion

Forget Xanax, Listen to the Spin Doctors

The Manly Art of Teabagging

Mouse Versus Scorpion: The Ultimate Showdown

I'm Not a Dumpster Diver, I'm a Trash Whisperer

Rock, Flag, Eagle: How to Rise Up and Kick Some Ass

Tips on Caring for Your Bison Fingers

Making Friends Through Lies and Manipulation

Going Green: How to Run Your Bar on Trash

The "It Doesn't Get Better" Project

How to Make Sweet Love to Her . . . Without Waking Her

The Cream Always Rises to the Top

Huff This, Don't Huff That!

Illiteracy: What It *Really* Means

The Art of the Ocular Pat-Down

The Chalupa: Your Tool for Tacking on Mass

Full-On Rapist or Philanthropist? The Dos and Don'ts of Online
Dating

Coming soon to wherever they still sell books. They still sell books, right? I think there's a place downtown by the buggy whip store.

ACKNOWLEDGMENTS

The gang would like to acknowledge—or, better yet, have the world at large acknowledge—that without our tireless efforts and dogged determination, this very important book would not have happened. And if this book had not happened, a lot of really messed-up people would not have gotten the help they needed from us, not wanted to go on living anymore, and probably have killed themselves. Or worse yet, not killed themselves. Because the only thing worse than someone not getting the help they need is to just keep hanging around like a sad sack forever. It's like wiping down the glory hole after you use it. Just good manners.

Beyond us, there really aren't many people who deserve any credit for this book. Well, there's this one guy who comes in the bar all the time named Dan. Last name's Dunn or O'Dumb or Dunce . . . something Irish. Anyway, it turns out this Dunce guy knows a thing or two about writing. Took a bunch of community college English classes or some shit. Anyway, he was around and when he heard we were doing a book he got all perky, so we wound up bouncing some ideas off him. Like, literally. We would write shit down on coasters and rolls of toilet paper and pool balls, and throw them at the dude. It really helped with the creative process.

While he was dodging cue balls, Dan would try to distract us by making up all this stuff about his "writing partner" Scott Alexander. Conveniently though, the guy never seemed to be around. Lives up in New York, Dan would say. Has all these kids. Sure he does, Dan. And how's your "Canadian girlfriend" doing?

Anyway, they kept bringing us all this crap they wrote and it's possible we unconsciously used an idea here or there or lifted a bunch of their stuff wholesale. Who can keep track when you're in the midst of a creative perfect storm? When the tsunami of truth comes for you, the last thing you're thinking about is making sure some imaginary jamoke up in Brooklyn gets credit for every precious word.

We'd also be remiss if we didn't thank the host of people who worked on this book. Thank you to: [REDACTED], whose overwhelming sexual attraction to Charlie and underwhelming alcohol tolerance scored us a book deal; [REDACTED], whose cover design made Dee look slightly less birdlike (like that's possible); [REDACTED], the sonofabitch copy editor who kept claiming that "jabroni" isn't a word; and our editor Brittany Hamblin, publicist Andy Dodds, and marketing team Michael Barrs and Shannon Donnelly (who are the only ones not trying to sue us, yet . . .). And of course special thanks to Damon Nightman for his editorial vision. (Ha . . . suck it, Dee!)

Thanks, guys. You couldn't have done it without us.